THE LIVERIES OF THE PRE-GROUPING

VOLUME FOUR

LONDON AND THE SOUTH OF ENGLAND

THE LIVERIES OF THE PRE-GROUPING RAILWAYS

VOLUME FOUR

LONDON AND THE SOUTH OF ENGLAND

NIGEL J.L. DIGBY

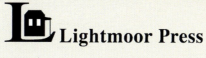

© Nigel J.L. Digby and Lightmoor Press 2020

Designed by Nigel Nicholson

British Library Cataloguing-in-Publication Data. A catalogue record for this book is available from the British Library

ISBN 9781 911038 82 5

All rights reserved. No part of this publication may be reproduced, stored in a retrieval system or transmitted in any form or by any means, electronic, mechanical, photocopying, recording or otherwise, without the written permission of the publisher

LIGHTMOOR PRESS

Unit 144B, Lydney Trading Estate, Harbour Road, Lydney, Gloucestershire GL15 4EJ

www.lightmoor.co.uk

Lightmoor Press is an imprint of Black Dwarf Lightmoor Publications Ltd

Printed in Poland; www.lfbookservices.co.uk

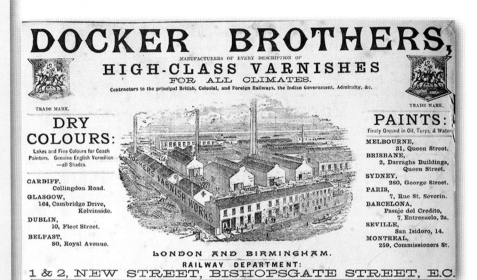

London Tilbury & Southend Railway 4-4-2T No. 47 *Stratford* runs into Barking station in 1909 on a Southend service, passing District Railway Class 'B' No. 124 waiting at the other platform with an Ealing train. *Author's collection*

Contents

Introduction	*310*
London & South Western Railway	311
London Brighton & South Coast Railway (to 1904)	321
London Brighton & South Coast Railway (from 1905)	329
London Chatham & Dover Railway	337
London Tilbury & Southend Railway	345
Metropolitan District Railway	351
Metropolitan Railway	361
North London Railway	373
Somerset & Dorset Joint Railway	381
South Eastern & Chatham Railway	391
South Eastern Railway	399
Acknowledgments	*408*
Bibliography	*408*

Railway Companies in Previous Volumes

Volume 1
Wales and the West of England
Barry
Brecon & Merthyr
Cambrian
Great Western (1882-1904)
Great Western (1905-1922)
Mersey
Midland & South Western Junction
Rhondda & Swansea Bay
Rhymney
Taff Vale
Wirral
Wrexham, Mold & Connah's Quay

Volume 2
The East of England and Scotland
Colne Valley & Halstead
Great Central
Great Eastern
Great Northern
Great North of Scotland
Hull & Barnsley
Lancashire, Derbyshire & East Coast
Manchester, Sheffield & Lincolnshire
Midland & Great Northern Joint
Mid-Suffolk Light
North British
North Eastern

Volume 3
The North of England and Scotland
Caledonian
Cheshire Lines Committee
Furness
Glasgow & South Western
Highland (to 1902)
Highland (from 1902)
Lancashire & Yorkshire
London & North Western
Maryport & Carlisle
Midland (to 1906)
Midland (1906-22)
North Staffordshire
Stratford-upon-Avon & Midland Junction

Introduction to Volume Four

This final volume deals with the standard gauge railways in the south of England, and those associated with London. Many of them became constituents of the Southern Railway in 1923, but the North London Railway and the London Tilbury & Southend Railway were constituents of the London Midland & Scottish Railway, and the Metropolitan Railway and the District Railway remained independent until they were absorbed into the London Passenger Transport Board in 1933. The Somerset & Dorset Joint Railway was jointly administered by the SR and the LM&SR.

Upon Nationalisation in 1948, the SR became the Southern Region of British Railways, and the NLR and LT&SR sections of the LM&SR became part of the London Midland Region, but the LT&SR was made over to the Eastern Region in the following year. The S&DJR was retained as part of the Southern Region, but the northern section was transferred to the Western Region in 1958.

For this volume further sketches, paintings and contemporary postcards and prints have been added. I have also revised some paintings and their text according to new information received.

Where possible, the colours are given references. The first [Carter] is from the colour chart in E.F. Carter's *Britain's Railway Liveries*. The second reference [Pantone C] is from the Pantone PMS formula guide (coated). The third [BS] is from the British Standard colour charts of which there are several. Occasionally, where there is no close match to these charts, the European RAL standard has been employed. I have not included Munsell references, as it is almost impossible to get physical access to a Munsell chart, whereas the others are readily available to order online. Rather than interrupt the flow of the text, the colour references are shown as footnotes. However, where I have good reason to believe a colour is a good match, but have no documentary evidence to prove it, I have mentioned this in the body of the text.

While the shades printed here cannot be taken as gospel, colour printing not being an exact process, the British Standard colour information and the Pantone or RAL swatches are less vulnerable to variation and form a stable point of reference. It should be borne in mind that these colours are the ones that I suggest were applied to the full-sized object. For use on models they must be lightened, or their small surface area will give an impression that is too dark.

Every work such as this has its errors, despite the best efforts of all concerned, which have been brought to my attention by readers, or I have noticed myself. There are inevitably a few typographical mistakes, but I have brought together the most noticeable errors in the paintings and presented them again in their corrected form.

At the end of this volume are the acknowledgements, both of individuals and of societies, who have assisted me greatly in the mammoth task that I set myself in 1994. There is also a bibliography, which I am pleased to say has increased in recent years, there being many more books dedicated to this fascinating and important subject.

Nigel Digby
Cromer 2020

North London Railway 0-6-0T No. 78 at Bow, 22nd August 1901.

Author's collection

London & South Western Railway

The London & South Western Railway could claim to be the most senior railway west of London. It was promoted in 1831 under the name Southampton, London and Branch Railway and Dock Company, for a line between London (Nine Elms) and Southampton. The docks at Southampton were transferred to a separate undertaking and the London & Southampton Railway obtained its Act of Parliament in 1834. The railway opened its first section in 1838, but constructional difficulties meant that the line was not opened in its entirety until 1840.

A branch to Gosport near Portsmouth was authorised in 1839, and it was to placate the inhabitants of that town that the railway changed its name to the London & South Western Railway at the same time. The line opened from Bishopstoke Junction in 1842, renamed Eastleigh & Bishopstoke in 1889, and Eastleigh in 1923.

Further expansion westwards was a continuous battle with the Great Western Railway broad gauge interests. The Southampton to Dorchester line opened in 1847, Salisbury was reached via Bishopstoke Junction in 1847, and more directly via Andover in 1857. Finally, the L&SWR reached Yeovil and Exeter (Queen Street) in 1860.

To give the railway a more convenient London terminus, an extension to a large new station at Waterloo was opened in 1848. The site at Nine Elms remained as a goods station, locomotive shed and engineering works. Also in London, the L&SWR built up a dense network of suburban lines and branches.

The L&SWR was determined to exploit Devon and Cornwall, acquiring the Exeter & Crediton Railway and the North Devon Railway in 1865, both originally broad gauge. A line from the North Devon Railway allowed working into Plymouth, and eventually spawned two routes to reach the north Cornwall coast at Bude (1898) and Padstow (1899), where the L&SWR finally joined the Bodmin & Wadebridge Railway which it had purchased in 1847.

Away from the main lines, the L&SWR consolidated its presence in the region by opening or absorbing several alternative routes and many branch lines. The L&SWR also purchased the Southampton Docks Company in 1892. Total mileage in 1901 was 793, with a further 28 jointly owned with the LB&SCR and the GWR. The L&SWR also participated with the Midland Railway in the third largest joint line in the country, the celebrated Somerset & Dorset Joint Railway (see later in this volume).

The engineering works of the L&SWR were originally on a site adjacent to Nine Elms in London. The area was found to be too cramped, so in 1891 the carriage and wagon department was moved to a new site adjacent to Bishopstoke & Eastleigh station, known simply as Eastleigh Works. The locomotive department was also moved to Eastleigh by the end of 1909.

The Locomotive Engineers of the L&SWR were Joseph Beattie (1850-71), W. George Beattie (1871-78), William Adams (1878-95), Dugald Drummond (1895-1912, styled as Chief Mechanical Engineer from 1904), and Robert Urie (1912-22).

The London & South Western Railway became a constituent of the Southern Railway in 1923, and passed into the Southern Region of British Railways in 1948.

The subject of L&SWR locomotive liveries is a complex one, much of which is before my period of reference. Indian red had been the base colour of locomotives under Mr Joseph Beattie

No. 343, from the Railway Magazine (September 1903). Author's collection

London & South Western Railway

from 1850 until circa 1859, when a very dark 'chocolate' brown was adopted. His son Mr W.G. Beattie preferred a slightly lighter chocolate colour.

When Mr William Adams took office as Locomotive Superintendent in 1878, a change in the locomotive colour was proposed. There were two alternatives, one an 'umber' brown, and the other a dark green. The brown was chosen, and adopted during 1879. Unfortunately the colour was found to be unsatisfactory, weathering badly, later called in *Moore's Monthly Magazine* (May 1896) a 'dirty brown'. Mr Adams was aware of this, and in 1883 began applying the alternative dark green livery. It seems he originally intended to use the dark green for all the locomotive stock, but was prevailed upon by the Locomotive Committee in 1885 to use a lighter green for the principal passenger locomotives, extended to all passenger locomotives in 1887. The dark green remained in use on goods locomotives until the end of the L&SWR.

The 'light green', as it was often specified [1], was also described as 'pea' green or 'light grass' green. Lining was confined to boiler bands and panel edges, including the cab front, being a 3-inch black band edged with a thin 3/16-inch white line, and corners were radiused rather than square. The width of the black edging was reduced where necessary on smaller panels and when beside brass beading.

A surviving specification calls for the usual surface preparation, followed by two coats of lead colour, then two coats of light green. The outside of frames, guard irons, tops of splashers, smokebox, chimney, cab roof, back of firebox, ashpan, footplate, brake work, side springs, and top and bottom of tender were to receive one coat of lead colour and two coats of black japan. The insides of frames

J.H. Beattie's 'Vesuvius' Class 2-4-0 No. 14 *Mercury* is seen before being rebuilt by Adams. The thirty-two members of this class were built at Nine Elms 1869-75 and withdrawn 1893-99.
Author's collection

Adams locomotive livery.

London & South Western Railway

were to have one coat of red oxide and one coat of 'tan colour'. The outside of the engine was to be finished with three coats of copal varnish.

Bufferbeams and buffer casings were vermilion [2], the engine number being applied in the usual way, for example "Nº [hook] 462" in 4½-inch gilt characters shaded in black. Cut-out brass numerals were applied to cab side-sheets of tender locomotives, in the centres of side-tanks, and on the rear of the bunker of tank locomotives. There was no company identification.

Goods locomotives followed the same general pattern, but were painted two coats of a very dark olive green. A close equivalent is given by BS 381C 224 'Deep Bronze Green'. The black areas were just as for the light green engines, between the frames was tan colour, and bufferbeams and buffer casings were vermilion. Body panels followed the same lining scheme, except that white was replaced by light green.

Brass numerals to identify each locomotive were used until 1887 when elliptical brass numberplates were introduced on new construction. These were 23⅞ x 14⅞ inches, with a central number, "LONDON & SOUTH WESTERN RAILWAY C^{OY}" around the perimeter above, and "NINE ELMS WORKS [date]" below. The background was vermilion.

Company initials appeared at the same time, in 5¼-inch gold letters, shaded black. The first incarnation was "L & S W R", but within a few years the ampersand had been dropped and "L S W R" was being used, occupying 9 feet overall from centre to centre.

By 1890, a monogram made from the initials "LSWR" had appeared on the front splashers of express engines, rather small and plain until 1893, but larger and more florid thereafter.

When Mr Adams' successor Dugald Drummond took office, nothing was changed for about a year, but by May 1896 the livery was being altered, both in the lining style and in the locomotive colour. There is some dispute about the base colour, and some contemporary commentators maintained that the green did not change at all, but paint analysis seems to agree with other contemporary observers that the Drummond green [3] was slightly lighter and more yellow than the Adams green.

In all conscience, the greens are very similar. The formula for the Adams green, collected in *Southern Style, Part One* (John Harvey, HMRS), was Buckingham green in oil 4lb, zinc white in oil 2lb, lemon chrome in oil 1lb and a touch of drop black. The formula for the Drummond green is given as cypress (or royal) green in oil 4lb, zinc white in oil 2lb, lemon chrome in oil 1lb and drop black ¼lb. Royal green belongs to the Brunswick green group. The similarity between the two formulae is striking, the only significant difference being in the two green pigments.

Goods locomotive livery.

No. 395, from the Railway Magazine (November 1904). Author's collection

314
London & South Western Railway

No. 335, from the Railway Magazine (May 1909). Author's collection

315 London & South Western Railway

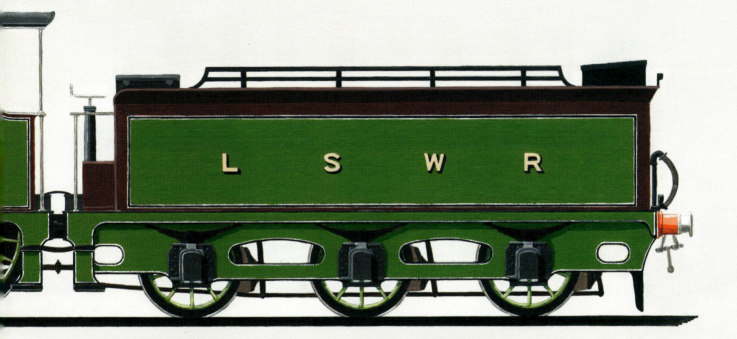

The major development of the Drummond livery was that all body and tender panels were edged with a broad band of 'purple brown' [4]. This was made up from purple brown in oil 6lb, burnt sienna in oil ¼lb and burnt umber in oil ¼lb. Lining was in black, separating the brown and the green, fine-lined in white. Lining now came together with right-angled corners or points, rather than curves as before. Boiler bands were also black, fine-lined in white, but with an equally-sized band of purple brown on the boiler clothing on each side.

Valances and tender frames did not feature purple brown, and were simply edged in black and white. Wheel tyres and axle ends were black, unlined. Bufferbeams were plain vermilion, outside faces of main frames were black, between the frames was tan colour, and the cab interior was painted buff and oak grained in the upper parts, and black below.

Engine numbers were on front and rear bufferbeams in the usual form, for example "N⁰ [hook] 706". The armorial device was applied to the forward splashers of 4-4-0s. This consisted of a shield bearing the arms of London, Southampton, Winchester, Portsmouth and Salisbury, surrounded by a blue garter carrying the words "LONDON & SOUTH WESTERN RAILWAY COMPANY". The crest was a dragon's wing, a feature that was replicated on many other company items.

Mr Drummond's earlier designs carried brass numberplates, apparently 17½ x 11 inches, lettered "South Western" above the number and "Railway" below. Unlike the larger Adams plates, the lettering was etched into the brass and filled with black, precisely the same as his design for the Caledonian Railway.

Following on from Mr Drummond's eccentric interpretation of the railway's title, tender and tank lettering was "S W R" in a new larger size of 8½ inches. From late 1897 to early 1898 the lettering used was "L S W", until he was prevailed upon finally to adopt the correct form "L S W R". The lettering on tenders was 12 feet 6 inches overall.

The brass plates remained unchanged, until they were abandoned about 1902 in favour of 6-inch gilt transfer numerals, shaded in black. With the transfer numerals, an unusual method was used to show engines on the duplicate list. At first a black line was struck through the middle of the number, superseded by a black line below the number. Finally a narrow gilt bar was placed below the number, treated in the same way as the main numerals. Previously a zero had been added to the front of the number and this method was eventually readopted.

Mr Drummond died in office and was succeeded by Robert Urie in 1912. At first there was no change, but apparently from December 1914 a softer, slightly olive green was adopted as the base

London & South Western Railway

colour, due to difficulties obtaining the original pigments. Often called 'sage' green, the equivalent is approximately BS 381C 219 'Sage Green'. The device was abandoned, and from October 1917 the lining was simplified to a black edging standardized at 3 inches wide, separated from the green by a thin white line, all corners being square.

Until William Panter was appointed Carriage & Wagon Superintendent in 1885, the carriage painting of the L&SWR seems to have been rather chaotic. Fortunately, the standard two-tone livery was introduced by the late 1880s and lasted, with minor adjustments, for over thirty years.

The standard method of carriage painting was recounted by Mr Panter's successor from 1906, Mr Surrey Warner, in *Railway Mechanical Engineering* (Gresham Publishing Company, 1923). Mr Warner's contribution to this fascinating and indispensable two-volume work harks back to practices before 1914.

It is at this point that the word 'salmon' is usually introduced to refer to the lighter colour applied to the waist panels and above. I refuse to use this nomenclature as it is subjective and very misleading. Research by the HMRS has amply shown that the colour, at least when fresh, was a light orange-brown. It actually closely resembles the 'teak colour' used on many other railways. Hamilton Ellis in his *South Western Railway* called it 'a light golden brown'.

Left: L&SWR carriage lining.

London & South Western Railway

Contemporary observers also found the colour difficult to pin down. *Moore's Monthly Magazine* refers to 'a light buff colour, with dark umber brown for the lower [panels]'. In the *Railway Magazine* (March 1901) a correspondent writes 'that peculiar blend of reddish yellow and Indian ink', the *Locomotive Magazine* (February 1903) refers to 'the lower portion dark chocolate, upper panels the usual buff colour', and in the *Railway Magazine* (October 1904) J.B. Baron Collins MA refers to an 'orangish [sic] salmon on upper panels and Worcester sauce lower panels'.

The lower colour, as can be inferred from the references to 'dark umber brown', 'dark chocolate', 'Indian ink' and Worcestershire sauce, was a dark brown. Mr Warner prosaically refers to it as 'brown', and the light orange upper colour as 'top colour'.

After the usual preparation coats, the entire upper portion of the carriage (waist panels, upright panels, eaves panels and all the fascia) were painted three coats of 'top colour' [5] followed by one coat of varnish top colour. The lower panels and the ends of the carriage were to be given two coats of lead colour, one coat of brown [6], and one coat of varnish brown colour. Solebars were to have one coat of lead colour, one coat of brown and one coat of varnish brown colour. Roofs were painted white lead, but the cornice was the body brown colour. Roof fittings were painted black.

Mr Warner refers to the lining colour as being 'dark-brown', which is odd, as it has been found to be indistinguishable from black on preserved carriage remains. The black was applied around the curved reveals of all the fascia (beading), there being a ⅛-inch vermilion fine-line between the lining and the top colour. The top edge of the bottom shell moulding was treated in the same way.

Droplight frames and quarter light (window) frames were painted 'mahogany colour', a red-brown equivalent. A reported peculiarity was the painting of the interior reveals of First Class quarter lights in yellow (probably lemon chrome) for identification purposes.

Below the solebars, brake gear, bogies and the like were black, except for Mansell wheel centres, which were varnished teak or 'mahogany colour'. Wheel tyres were white when newly out of shops. Steps and footboards were painted one coat of lead colour then one coat of black japan.

Lettering was in gold shaded in black, generally 2½ inches high over the gold. Until circa 1898 the initials were in the form "L & S W R", thereafter the ampersand was dropped. The company initials "LSWR" were now about 18 inches in overall length. The usual arrangement on shorter passenger vehicles was to have "LSWR" in the panels to the left, with the number in a corresponding position on the right. Longer bogie vehicles used a symmetrical arrangement, with "LSWR" in the centre, and two numbers disposed at an equal distance on each side. Brake vehicles with a central ducket usually had the number on the upright panels and "LSWR" on the waist panel below.

Class marking was in words "FIRST", "SECOND" or "THIRD" on the waist panel of each door. For the new fixed sets of bogie suburban carriages in 1903, large 12-inch gold seriffed class numerals were used on the bottom panels of the doors for ease of

London & South Western Railway

L&SWR 4-6-0 No. 443 heads the Down Bournemouth Express, near Esher. *Author's collection*

identification. Within a few years, these had been superseded by "1ST", "2ND" and "3RD" in the waist panel.

Other lettering was "GUARD" on a single door and "GUARDS | COMPT" on double doors, or "LUGGAGE | COMPT". For all of this class marking and subsidiary lettering, the initial letter was slightly larger than the 2½-inch standard.

From 1912 the company initials and number were now applied in characters 4½ inches high, with the initials and a single number placed closer together near the middle of the coach. Other lettering remained unaltered, except that Second class was abolished in 1918.

It should be mentioned that during the 1914-18 war, the carriage colours noticeably changed. The top colour took on a distinctly 'terracotta' shade and the lower panels assumed a strange greenish-black aspect. It is assumed that this was because of the difficulty of obtaining the pigments, and it is believed that any surviving mixing formulae date from this time as a way of approximating the earlier standard livery.

Non-passenger coaching vehicles (carriage trucks, horseboxes and so on) were coach brown all over, except milk vans which were carriage 'top colour' all over from at least 1907, with the standard lining.

The L&SWR electrified a considerable amount of its suburban system and new electric stock was constructed ready for the start of electric services in 1915. Green was adopted for this electric stock, applied in a single colour to all the carriages. Recent research has shown that this was a dark green. Solebars and carriage ends were black, except for the driving ends, which were treated in the same way as the sides. The lining scheme followed the same format as the two-tone carriages, with black on the reveals of the fascia, but the ⅛-inch fine-lining was now in yellow. This new scheme was applied generally to all the carriage stock in 1921 and was adopted as standard by the Southern Railway in 1923.

From 1880, goods stock was painted a dark brown, a standard that continued until the end of the L&SWR. It was apparently called 'Richmond brown' and was obtained from the manufacturers Denton & Jutsum. It was applied to all of the wagon including timber underframes, but steel underframes were black japan. The later Southern Railway wagon colour was very similar to the L&SWR brown, and this was given by a 5:4 mix of burnt umber and raw umber. Body ironwork was black japanned. Interiors of open wagons were lead colour; floors of vans were also lead colour but interior walls were white, as were van roofs. The ends of brake vans and 'road vans' were painted red, believed to be Venetian red rather than vermilion.

Lettering during the Adams period was small, about 6 inches, and in the form "L&SWR [door] (number)" on each side of open wagon doors. On van doors the number was painted below the initials. From circa 1891 large lettering was introduced, nominally 12 inches but varying to fit circumstances. Open wagons were lettered "L S [door] W R", but vans, which usually had outside framing had

319 London & South Western Railway

ABOVE: L&SWR 32ft milk van No. 163, seen in all-over carriage 'top colour'; it was built at Eastleigh in June 1907 and withdrawn November 1941 as SR No. 1641.
Author's collection

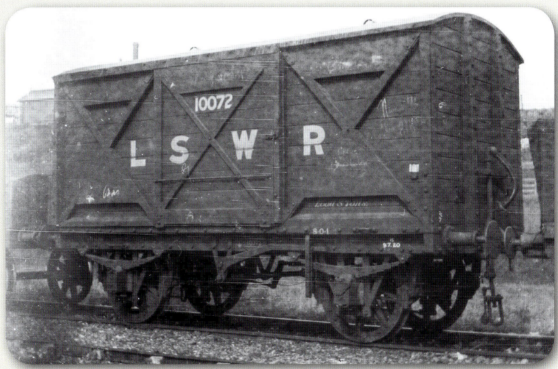

L&SWR 8-ton box van No. 10072 is seen in the late 1920s.
Author's collection

the middle two initials on the door, for example "L [S W] R". The number was on the door above the initials. Open wagons had their numbers painted on the lower right. Note that the outside strokes of the "W" were curved, rather than straight.

On the solebar was a large elliptical numberplate, 13¼ x 7¼ inches, with the wagon number central. Over it was "L&SWRCº", with the place of construction below, latterly being "EASTLEIGH WORKS".

The only exceptions to the dark brown standard were the refrigerator vans. From at least 1907, these were painted a light colour, apparently with red initials. There has been controversy about this colour but, for the record, Mr Warner specifies that these vans were painted 'a light stone colour'. This is a light yellowish brown colour, based on white, yellow ochre and burnt umber, for which something like BS 381C 361 'Light Stone' would seem to be indicated.

320 London & South Western Railway

Service vehicles and departmental stock were painted red oxide, lettered as for the revenue wagons, but usually with the addition of "ENGINEER'S DEPARTMENT" in small white letters.

Wagon sheets were standardised at 21ft 4ins x 15ft 4ins. The earliest form was to have "LSWRCº" painted in an arc on each side of the sheet, apparently succeeded by a simple "L&SWR" in 24-inch letters taking up each long side. From about 1895 the standard form was "LSWR" in 18-inch letters on each long side with the number in a smaller 10-inch size below. Small-sized initials "LSWR" were placed across the middle of the sheet between the main lettering, or alternatively at each end, and small numbers could also appear at each corner.

Note that in light of the exemplary work on this subject by the HMRS, I have adjusted some of the Carter colour references below.

1 'ADAMS GREEN'
CARTER 7
PANTONE 7742C
RAL 6010
'GRASS GREEN'

2 'VERMILION'
CARTER 36
PANTONE 485C
BS 4800 04 E 53
'POPPY RED'

3 'DRUMMOND GREEN'
CARTER 2
PANTONE 2278C
BS 381C 218
'GRASS GREEN'

4 'PURPLE BROWN'
CARTER 29
PANTONE 483C
BS 381C 448
'DEEP INDIAN RED'

5 'CARRIAGE TOP COLOUR'
CARTER 48
PANTONE 7566C
BS 5252 06 D 44

6 'CARRIAGE BROWN'
CARTER 39
PANTONE 2322C
BS 5252 06 C 40

London Brighton & South Coast Railway (to 1904)

The London Brighton & South Coast Railway was formed by amalgamation of the London & Croydon and London & Brighton railways in July 1846. The London & Croydon Railway was the older partner, being incorporated in 1835. Opened in 1839, Croydon trains ran from London Bridge station, sharing the route with the London & Greenwich Railway from which they diverged at Corbett's Lane Junction. From there, the L&CR ran to Croydon over the route of the moribund Croydon Canal, which it had purchased.

The London & Brighton Railway was incorporated in 1837, for a line from a junction at Norwood on the L&CR, direct to Brighton via Redhill and Hayward's Heath. The line had been approved with the proviso that the South Eastern Railway was also to use it as their approach to London, from a junction at Redhill. The Brighton line was opened throughout in 1841. The first section of the SER opened from Tonbridge to Redhill in 1842. The SER paid the L&BR £340,000 in 1844 to purchase half of the line, as it was entitled to do, and they were sold the section from Redhill to Coulsdon. The line from Norwood to Redhill was still worked by both companies, but in practice SER and LB&SCR trains only stopped at stations on their own parts of the line.

So closely did the railways work that for a few years there was a joint locomotive and rolling stock committee between the London & Croydon, South Eastern and London & Brighton railways, but this was dissolved in January 1846 and in July the LB&SCR was formed.

Over the succeeding years, the LB&SCR opened lines along the coast to Portsmouth in the west, and to Eastbourne, Newhaven and Hastings in the east. Inland, new through lines and branches were opened throughout Sussex and Surrey, so that the LB&SCR covered a large triangular area with its base on the south coast and its apex in London. The second London terminus, Victoria, was opened in 1860, although the company offices remained at London Bridge.

The shared line between Redhill and Croydon became an irritating bottleneck, and to avoid it the LB&SCR opened an independent parallel route in 1900.

Around South London, a dense system of suburban lines was evolved, originally centred around the rebuilt Crystal Palace at Sydenham, but then expanding outward. The loop between London Bridge and Victoria was electrified with great success in 1909, using the overhead system. More suburban routes followed and the company was investigating the possibility of electrifying the main line to Brighton when the First World War intervened.

In 1901, the LB&SCR owned a mileage of 431 miles, with a further 38 jointly owned. The company had several miles jointly with its neighbour the L&SWR, including the Portsmouth, Southsea & Ryde, and participated in two very important cross-London lines, the West London Extension Railway and the East London Railway.

The LB&SCR's engineering works were established at Brighton in 1840. The cramped site encouraged the company to open a separate carriage and wagon works at Lancing near Shoreham-by-Sea in 1909.

The Locomotive, Carriage and Wagon Superintendents of the LB&SCR in this earlier period were John Chester Craven (1846-70), William Stroudley (1870-89) and Robert J. Billinton (1890-1904).

Under Mr Craven, the livery of LB&SCR locomotives was by no means standardised, but the majority of engines were Brunswick green with 'crimson lake' frames and splashers. Lining is believed to have been black, fine-lined white, body panels of lining having incurved corners. There was a great deal of polished brass and copper.

When William Stroudley was appointed, he brought with him a distinctive livery from the Highland Railway. This was based upon a strange greenish brown, with a darker green border and elaborate

No. 43 *Duchess of Fyfe*, from the Railway Magazine (April 1903). Author's collection

322
London Brighton & South Coast Railway (to 1904)

The 'Brighton Express'. Author's collection

London Brighton & South Coast Railway (to 1904)

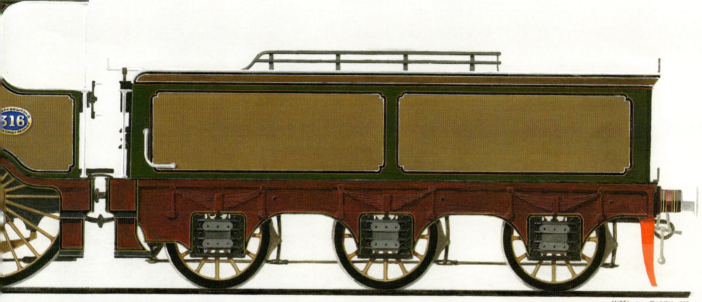

lining. In April 1870 Mr Stroudley had one engine painted in what he considered an improved shade for the Directors to approve. This new colour has been described variously as 'dark yellow', 'yellow' and 'golden ochre', but Mr Stroudley, and by extension the paint shop, always referred to it as 'Improved Engine Green'. On specification documents (confusingly) it is simply referred to as 'green'. Yellow is often favoured as a convenient label, but it was actually a light brown. In this chapter, for brevity and to avoid confusion with actual chrome yellow, I will refer to it as 'ochre'.

Stroudley's ochre for passenger engines was based on Oxford ochre. There is no mystery about this pigment, it was a high-quality yellow ochre (hydrated iron III oxide with silica and alumina) found in a seam in the Shotover Hills, Oxfordshire. This seam had been worked since mediaeval times, yellow ochre being one of the oldest pigments used for decorative purposes.

In the paint shop at Brighton, the natural colour of the yellow ochre, which being a fine grade was quite dark, was modified by mixing it with iron oxide (Indian red), chrome yellow and lead white to a greenish yellow-brown [1].

The boiler, dome, tanks, tender sides, cabs, splashers, sandboxes, indeed all panels above the platform (footplate) were painted ochre. Smokeboxes, chimneys, platform, cylinder covers, tank tops and splasher tops were black. Chimneys had polished copper caps.

All the ochre panels were bordered with a dark olive green [2], tenders being divided into two panels by an olive green vertical. Between the two colours was a band of lining, consisting of 1½ inches of black, edged on the outside by a ⅛-inch vermilion line [3] and on the inside by a ⅛-inch white line. Boiler bands were black, edged with a ⅛-inch vermilion line, bordered on each side by a 2-inch olive green band edged with a ⅛-inch white line.

Standard Stroudley passenger locomotive bufferbeam.

London Brighton & South Coast Railway (to 1904)

LB&SCR Class 'D2' No. 312 *Albion*. Built in September 1883, it was renumbered as 612 in March 1905.   Author's collection

A typical LB&SCR express train. Note the vermilion end of the brake van.   Author's collection

Footplate valances and steps, outside frames, buffer beams, buffer housings and coupling rods were crimson lake [4]. The outer edge of valancing and frames was lined with yellow, black and vermilion, as were the buffer housings. The buffer beam had a central panel of vermilion, surrounded with a cartouche of white, black, yellow, black and vermilion lines. Billinton simplified this to white, black and yellow. Guard irons, sand pipes and interior faces of frames were vermilion, exterior faces of inside frames being black. Although wheels were ochre, axle ends and balance weights were olive green and tyres were black. An unusual feature was the continuation of the line of the spokes in ochre across the balance weights.

Goods locomotives were dark olive green lined with plain black bands. Those engines fitted with the Westinghouse brake had the lining edged with vermilion. There were of course variations but this mostly held true. Buffer beams and buffer sockets were vermilion, lined with white, black and yellow, and guard irons were also vermilion. Wheels, outside frames, coupling rods and interiors of cabs were olive green. Inside frames, wheel tyres and balance weights were black, and the lines of the spokes were carried across the balance weights in green.

Numberplates were elliptical brass, the recessed area around the numbers being painted blue. The wide border had the full name of the company etched into it, the letters being black. There was no other company designation on locomotives during this period, although passenger engines were named. The lettering for the names was in gold, blocked in 'sea green' and shadowed in black. The green blocking was highlighted in white and shaded underneath in crimson. After 1884 the shed allocation was painted in small white block letters on the front end of the footplate valances. The shed names were abbreviated, for example B = Battersea, B'TON = Brighton, N+ = New Cross.

Passenger vehicles were originally varnished mahogany [5]. A

London Brighton & South Coast Railway (to 1904)

No. 175 *Hayling*, built by Mr Stroudley in 1890 as one of the thirty-six Class 'B1' express locomotives. *Author's collection*

A rare clear view of the goods livery. Class 'E6' No. 411 *Blackheath* was introduced to traffic in May 1905, the livery following that of earlier members of the class. Its name was removed in November 1911 when it was reclassified as 'E6x'. *Author's collection*

10 inches diameter blue garter bearing the company name was placed centrally on the lower body of all coaches, and until circa 1898 the running number was placed within this garter in ornately seriffed numerals. Lining had been gilt, but by the 1890s was yellow around all panels. Brake ends were vermilion, roofs and wheel rims when new were white. Lettering was confined to class marking on each door, being gold sans-serif characters highlighted in white.

Carriage livery experiments commenced in the 1890s, when a number of individual carriages and at least one complete seven-car bogie train were subject to a number of colour combinations which were duly recorded in *The Locomotive Magazine*. Eventually in 1903 the combination of white upper panels and umber [6] lower panels lined with gold was chosen. The result was quite smart when new but weathering gave the upper panels an off-white tinge.

Another experiment in 1897 saw 6-wheeled First No. 569 painted with lower panels olive green and the upper ones white

LB&SCR. Goods locomotive livery, unfitted engines.

326 London Brighton & South Coast Railway (to 1904)

with a tinge of green. There were gold stripes around the panels with finer vermilion lines on either side. The lettering was in gold with red and green shading, while the underframe was picked out in yellow and a coat of arms was placed in the bottom quarter panel.

In 1901 bogie carriage No. 23 was finished in dark green for the lower panels and white just tinted with green for the upper panels, and lined in yellow with a fine vermilion line to separate from the dark green. This appears to be a slight variation of the 1897 experiment.

There were several other experiments at the same time.

Non-passenger carrying stock was painted mahogany without lining, lettered on two lines in white. The initials "L.B.& S.C.R." were centred on the body or main door of the vehicle, with the number below prefixed by "Nº". During the Billinton period, the number appeared without a prefix.

Goods stock was originally light grey with black ironwork on body and underframe. The grey seems to have been similar to Midland grey, darkening on exposure to the atmosphere. Company designation was confined to the elliptical numberplate on the solebar, but each vehicle had a circular symbol at the upper left, with the number below in 3-inch white numerals. The two common types of open wagons, types 'A' and 'D', also had an appropriate

Early wagon lettering, type 'A' open wagon.

327
London Brighton & South Coast Railway (to 1904)

LB&SCR van No. 8205. Author's collection

London Brighton & South Coast Railway (to 1904)

letter placed over the number, to the left of the symbol. This symbol consisted of a 9-inch blue circle containing a white shield on which was a red cross.

From about 1895 the grey used was darkened to a medium shade, the symbol was abandoned and body lettering appeared in approximately 7½-inch characters in the form "LB&SCR", although there was a short period when the R was expanded to "R^Y". The number still appeared to the left in 3-inch numerals with the type letter above. From about 1903 the company letters increased in size to 9 inches, with numbers to the left in 6 inches, and type letters were dropped. Brake vans had the company letters in the upper part of the side with the number below of equal size. Their ends were painted vermilion.

Wagon sheets were lettered and numbered in white on the longer sides in large 18-inch characters "LB&SCR" with the number below. A diagonal cross occupied the middle portion of the sheet.

1	'Improved Engine Green' Carter 33 Pantone 464C BS 5252 08 D 45
2	'Olive Green' Carter 4 Pantone 5747C BS 381C 223 'Mid Bronze Green'
3	'Vermilion' Carter 36 Pantone 485C BS 4800 04 E 53 'Poppy Red'
4	'Crimson' Carter 28 Pantone 188C BS 381C 540 'Crimson'
5	'Mahogany' Carter 44 Pantone 175C RAL 8015 'Chestnut Brown'
6	'Raw Umber' Carter 44 Pantone 175C BS 4800 06 C 40

London Brighton & South Coast Railway (from 1905)

The locomotive liveries of the LB&SCR were in two major periods. The most well-known is that introduced in 1870 by William Stroudley and continued by his successor Robert Billinton; this was dealt with in the previous chapter. The change to the second-period umber livery covered in this chapter occurred under Douglas Earle Marsh (1904-11) and was maintained until the Grouping by Lawson B. Billinton (1912-22).

The LB&SCR became a constituent of the Southern Railway in 1923 and passed into the Southern Region of British Railways in 1948.

Although there had been rumours of a change in locomotive livery all through 1905, it was not until December of that year that the first examples of the new Marsh passenger locomotive livery appeared. The main body colour was raw umber [1]; a cool, greenish brown. This was applied to boiler, tanksides, cabs and tenders. A darker shade of umber brown [2] was used to border the tanks, tenders, cabs and bunkers. Between the two colours was a black band forming panels with incurved corners.

One reason for the change may have been cost. The Oxford Ochre at the time was reported as being 'exhausted'.

The fine-lining colour depended on the class of engine. The express locomotives, for example the Class 'B4' 4-4-0s, are reported to have had 'gold' fine-lining, which seems unlikely to be literally true. It was probably an equivalent 'gold colour', a practice employed by painters and signwriters to this day. Ordinary passenger engines had chrome yellow fine-lining. The dark brown was also applied to frames above the footplate and valances and steps. This was edged with black and fine-lined with the appropriate colour. Wheels were the dark brown, and tyres and axle ends were black.

How this darker shade of brown was produced is not known, but it reportedly had a greenish hue. Common sense suggests this secondary colour may simply have been burnt umber. Contemporary postcards, based on the paintings of 'F. Moore', seem to ignore the two-tone aspects of Marsh's livery and depict the whole engine in burnt umber – the *Locomotive Magazine* plates are much better. Main frames were black, and between the frames was vermilion. Cab roofs also seem to have been black.

The umber engines were now lettered "L B & S C R" on tanks or tenders in about 7½-inch gold characters, shaded in black to right and below. Names were mostly abandoned, although a few select locomotives retained them, the characters being in gold, shaded black. The old elliptical numberplates, which had a polished brass border carrying the name of the company around the central number, were at first retained. The background was now black instead of blue as formerly. After a short time, however, it became usual to apply gold transfer numerals instead. Express locomotives had a monogram of the company initials "LB&SCR" placed on the driving wheel splasher, or in the case of the Marsh Atlantics, on both splashers. For a short time, the monogram was very elaborate, but by 1906 had been simplified. This monogram used entwined letters of various sizes with "L B" the most prominent, all in gold shaded with black.

The bufferbeams were very different from the former Stroudley/Billinton standard. They were now simply painted vermilion and

No. 37, from the Railway Magazine (June 1906). Author's collection

330
London Brighton & South Coast Railway (from 1905)

No. 321, from the Railway Magazine (April 1911). Author's collection

London Brighton & South Coast Railway (from 1905)

carried the engine number in the usual form, "Nº [hook] 29" for example, in gold shaded in black. Buffer casings were dark brown, lined on the outer lip. The home depot was painted in tiny white letters just behind the bufferbeam until the later changes.

Goods locomotives were now painted black instead of olive green, and lining was in two parallel vermilion lines following the same form as on the umber engines. The old standard numberplates were retained at first, now with vermilion backgrounds, but after a short time transfers were used. Bufferbeams were vermilion with the usual numbering. All lettering was in yellow, shaded in red and highlighted in white.

When Mr Lawson Billinton succeeded Mr Marsh in 1912, the overall livery styles remained, but the favoured lettering on tanks and tenders now became simply "L B S C", although some engines still had the older lettering in 1922. The size of the lettering increased to about 10 inches at first, but subsequently to 12 inches. Any surviving numberplates were removed, replaced by transfer numerals of the same size as the main lettering. 'Gold' lining on express types was replaced by chrome yellow, and the monograms were abandoned, although the old elaborate 1881 device appeared on some engines.

An unusual feature of these years was the number of occasions in which locomotives remained painted in photographic grey for some considerable time. Class 'I3' 4-4-2T No. 22 of 1908, Class 'J1' 4-6-2T No. 325 *Abergavenny* of 1910, Class 'H2' 4-4-2 No. 421 of 1911 and Class 'L' 4-6-4T No. 327 *Charles C. Macrae* of 1914 all ran in this form. Another Class 'L', No. 333 *Remembrance*, appeared in grey in 1922 and never received the umber livery at all. This engine carried a bronze plaque commemorating all the LB&SCR employees lost in the war. Lining was black, fine-lined white, and lettering was white, shaded in black.

Just prior to Grouping, goods locomotives were being turned out in umber rather than black, apparently to use up stocks of paint. An interesting survivor was Class 'E5' 0-6-2T No. 591 *Tillington*, which reportedly retained the old Stroudley livery until 1917.

London Brighton & South Coast Railway (from 1905)

LB&SCR 'H1' Class 4-4-2 No. 37, built in 1905. *Author's collection*

LB&SCR 4-4-0 No. 314, originally named *Charles C. Macrae* when built in 1895. *Author's collection*

London Brighton & South Coast Railway (from 1905)

A typical contemporary postcard of incorrect colour: LB&SCR Class 'E5x' 0-6-2T No. 570. Designed by R.J. Billinton, it was rebuilt by D.E. Marsh in 1911.
Author's collection

LB&SCR Class 'I3' 4-4-2T No. 83, built in August 1912.
Author's collection

London Brighton & South Coast Railway (from 1905)

In the early years of the 20th century there were experiments with white and green, or olive green and ochre, two-tone carriage colours, and finally a new scheme was adopted to replace the original varnished mahogany and the red-brown 'mahogany' paint. In February 1903 the LB&SCR Board decided that new main line carriages, and those existing vehicles deemed worthy of main line use, should be painted raw umber on their lower panels and beading, and white on the upper panels. The white was tinted by the addition of a small quantity of raw umber, and of course the varnish would also have had a yellowing effect. Lining was ¼ inch wide, described variously as orange or straw (possibly a yellow ochre gold imitation) and followed the edges of the beading. New suburban carriages were painted raw umber only. The mahogany-coloured carriages persisted on local sets, until from about 1910 all vehicles were painted entirely raw umber [1], lined out around the beading as described above. This variety in method resulted in the three liveries being seen side-by-side, the subject of comment by the railway press in 1911, but the process of turning out all vehicles in umber had been completed by 1915.

Roofs were white. Solebars were probably the body colour at first, but black would have superseded this on bogie vehicles. Brake ends were painted vermilion until 1911, but ordinary carriage ends were umber, unlined. Door ventilators were umber, the ordinary ones being lined to represent louvres despite being flat. Smoking compartments had very prominent 'Anderson' ventilators and the word "SMOKING" in the eaves over the door and etched into the window glass to the right of the door.

Lettering on the umber-and-white stock was in gold, shaded in blue, shadowed in black. A symmetrical arrangement in the waist panels was preferred. On the bogie vehicles two numbers usually sandwiched two sets of initials, with doors and other panels intervening, for example: "number/LB&SCR/LB&SCR/number".

London Brighton & South Coast Railway (from 1905)

Six-wheeled vehicles with five compartments had exactly the same arrangement, but those with four had the initials centrally, with two numbers on the panels on either side. When the company initials were first introduced, full stops were used between the letters, but this practice was not continued. The letters were spaced out to fill the entire panel. Class marking was in words "FIRST", "SECOND" or "THIRD" in the waist of the doors.

Lettering on the all-umber stock followed exactly the same pattern as detailed above, but was in gold shaded in black only. By about 1915, the initials had been simplified to "L B S C".

Goods wagons were painted a light medium grey, and had been since 1895. Body ironwork was often painted black. From 1903 the lettering had been "LB&SCR" in 9-inch white characters, arranged across the sides and doors of open wagons and vans thus: "L [B&SC] R", with the central portion on the door. The wagon number was painted in 6-inch numerals to the lower left of open wagons and upper left of vans. Brake vans had the company initials on the upper part of the side, with the number centrally below in equal size numerals. An elliptical numberplate was placed on the solebars, with "LONDON BRIGHTON AND" over, and "SOUTH COAST RAILWAY" under the central number.

From 1911, the grey darkened to a medium shade, body ironwork was no longer painted black and the lettering was simplified. The initials were shortened to "L B S C" in 18-inch white letters, the middle two initials painted on the doors. Numbers were in 5-inch numerals, once again to the left. At the same time, a rectangular numberplate was favoured on new stock, with simply "LBSC" over the number, and the permissible load between, for example "8 TONS".

Wagon sheets were lettered on each long side in large 18-inch characters "LB&SCR", with the number below also in 18-inch numerals. The centre of the sheet carried a diagonal white cross. After 1911, the initials were probably shortened to "LBSC".

336
London Brighton & South Coast Railway (from 1905)

1 'Umber'
Carter 44
Pantone 175C
BS 4800 06 C 40

2 'Dark Umber'
BS 381C 437
'Very Dark Drab'

London Chatham & Dover Railway

The 'Chatham' was originally incorporated in 1853 as the East Kent Railway, for the construction of a line from Strood to Canterbury. This was meant to be an independent feeder line to the neighbouring South Eastern Railway. The first section of line to Faversham was opened in January 1858. The SER, however, was interested only in bankrupting the East Kent, forcing the latter into a more ambitious stance, and in 1859 the name was changed to the London Chatham & Dover Railway. The line to Canterbury was opened in 1860, followed by extensions to Dover in 1861 and the Kent Coast Railway to Ramsgate in 1863. Other incursions into SER territory were made throughout the 1860s and 1870s.

In London, the Victoria Station & Pimlico Railway was authorised in 1858, from Battersea across the Thames into the City of Westminster. This line had been promoted by the London Brighton & South Coast Railway, but was leased jointly to them, the Great Western Railway, the London & North Western Railway and the LC&DR. The 'Brighton' side of the station opened in 1860, the LC&DR connecting line opened in 1861 and the 'Chatham' side of the station opened in August 1862.

The LC&DR also had ambitions for a route into the City of London, the City Branch opening from Herne Hill to Elephant & Castle in 1862, Blackfriars Bridge (south of the river) in 1864, Ludgate Hill (north of the river) in 1865, and into Snow Hill tunnel to join up with the City Widened Lines of the Metropolitan Railway. Through services between the LC&DR and the Great Northern Railway began running in 1866. A short branch to a new terminus at Holborn Viaduct was opened in 1874. A second bridge was opened on the east side of the first in 1886 to serve a new station, St. Paul's (later renamed Blackfriars), and Blackfriars Bridge station was closed at the same time.

The rival Chatham and South Eastern railways indulged in cut-throat competition, with neither company having a high reputation among their customers. This was made doubly unpleasant by the enmity of the two Chairmen, James Staats Forbes and Edward (later Sir Edward) Watkin of the LC&DR and SER respectively. The situation improved after Watkin's resignation in 1894 and, under the leadership of SER Chairman Mr Henry Cosmo Orme Bonser, the unhealthy situation was resolved from 1st January 1899

In 1873 the LC&DR ordered four 2-4-0 'Europa' or 'C' Class locomotives from Sharpe, Stewart & Co. for use on the Continental mail trains. Seen here in green livery is Asia. It was numbered 54 by Kirtley and in 1892 was rebuilt and painted black.

Author's collection

London Chatham & Dover Railway

by the formation of the South Eastern and Chatham Railways Joint Managing Committee, known operationally as the South Eastern & Chatham Railway.

The Locomotive, Carriage and Wagon Superintendents of the LC&DR were William Martley (1860-74) and William Kirtley (1874-98), nephew of Matthew Kirtley of the Midland Railway. Before Mr Martley's appointment, the Locomotive Committee had been advised by Thomas Russell Crampton, who despite his many other achievements must remain one of the worst locomotive engineers the Victorian period ever produced. The disastrous results took several years to rectify.

The LC&DR engineering works were established in 1862 at Longhedge, near Battersea in London. They constructed several locomotives and rebuilt many for Mr Martley, but it was under William Kirtley that Longhedge really came into its own. Sadly, after 1904 it was used only for heavy repairs, and in 1911 much of the plant was transferred to Ashford, the main works of the SE&CR.

On the 31st December 1898, the LC&DR had a route mileage of 189 miles, plus a further 8½ miles jointly with the SER (the Dover & Deal Joint). The company, although jointly managed as the SE&CR, retained its legal identity and became a constituent of the Southern Railway in 1923, passing into the Southern Region of British Railways in 1948.

On his arrival on the LC&DR from his previous post on the Great Western Railway, Mr Martley found that the only locomotives available were the 'Sondes' Class 4-4-0STs designed by Crampton, which he had to withdraw as soon as possible (they were broken up in 1865). Because replacement locomotives already ordered from the builders were not ready, Mr Martley had no choice but to scour the country looking for locomotives to buy cheaply or hire, which he did from other railway companies and locomotive builders. For example, he came across an order of four new engines originally built for export to South America, which became the 'Aeolus' Class.

When the Crampton-designed engines finally arrived in 1861-2, they were as bad as could be expected. Mr Martley had to rebuild them all and the new works at Longhedge was kept busy with this work for several years. Fortunately he had been ordering new locomotives of his own design from outside contractors, and by the end of his tenure the railway had a supply of very useful and

London Chatham & Dover Railway

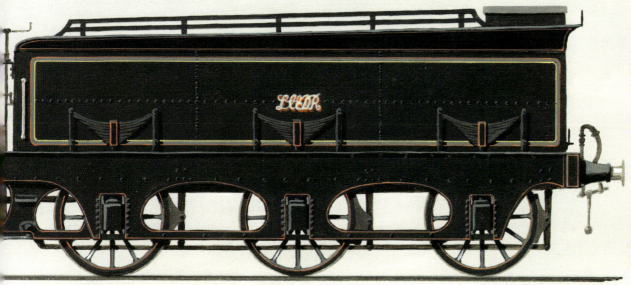

often remarkable machines. Possibly the best known are his 'Large Scotchmen' Class 0-4-2WTs for suburban work and his 'Europa' Class 2-4-0s for the fast mail trains to Dover.

The LC&DR favoured green as the standard locomotive colour. This was a medium-dark chrome green [1], similar to the later Great Central Railway green. Most locomotives had outside frames below the platform (footplate), and these were a dark red-brown described as 'chocolate' [2]. Wheels were green with black tyres. Bufferbeams were vermilion.

There were a few departures from standard, namely the four

Standard locomotive bufferbeam.

London Chatham & Dover Railway

'Echo' Class 4-4-0 No. 31, formerly *Sylph*, was built as 4-2-0 with dummy crankshaft by Robert Stephenson & Co. in 1862. It was rebuilt to 4-4-0 in 1865 and the firebox replaced 1870-73. Kirtley placed it in the 'K' Class in 1875 and allocated the number 31. It was rebuilt again in April 1884 with new boiler and cylinders, and withdrawn October 1902. *Author's collection*

'Aeolus' Class 4-4-0s, which were delivered painted 'yellow', although I would say that this was almost certainly yellow ochre, or light brown, rather than actually chrome yellow. They would have been repainted green at their first visit to Longhedge.

At first it seems the lining consisted of plain black bands, but by the mid-1860s Mr Martley had settled on his own simple scheme. Boiler bands were black, and each body panel was edged with black. On the cab side sheets was an additional panel of black lining, with incurved corners, and tenders featured at least three of these panels. Even sandboxes received their panel of lining. Tanks were lined out with just the one large panel, again with incurved corners, and where the platform swept up in arcs to clear the outside cranks, the lining followed the shape precisely. All of the black was fine-lined with white; between the black of the panel edging and the green, and on each side of the panels of black lining to form bands 2 inches wide.

Below the platform, the chocolate framing was edged in black and fine-lined in vermilion [3]. Axle box fronts and spring buckles were also chocolate edged in black and vermilion. There is some doubt about the outside cranks to the driving wheels, but it is possible that they were vermilion.

Every engine was named, having a rectangular brass plate with the name in raised seriffed letters on a black background. The nameplates were fixed to the centre line of boilers just behind the smokebox, or centrally on tanksides. There was a great deal of polished brass and copper, including pipework, injectors, domes, safety valve covers, fillets between firebox and boiler, and beading to splashers, finished off with a polished copper chimney cap.

Sadly, Mr Martley died in office early in 1874. His successor was William Kirtley, formerly Works Manager at Derby, Midland Railway. Although the livery of his predecessor was maintained for the present, Mr Kirtley introduced several departures from previous practice. He preferred numbers to names and introduced a number list, classifying and numbering all existing locomotives, for which he designed an elliptical numberplate. The lettering "LONDON CHATHAM" was placed in small characters over the large seriffed number, with "& DOVER RAILWAY" below, on a black background. In addition, numbers were placed in large gold seriffed characters shaded in black on front and rear bufferbeams of all locomotives.

There was also a complete change in the design of LC&DR locomotives, first seen in Mr Kirtley's 'A' Class 0-4-4Ts of 1875, built by Neilson & Co. and the Vulcan Foundry. These engines abandoned the outside frames used for so long on the railway; their exposed wheels and enclosed domes with separate safety valves immediately gave them a more contemporary appearance than anything seen previously on the LC&DR. They also introduced 'Chatham' men to the unprecedented luxury of a roofed cab.

The 'A' Class 0-4-4Ts were painted in the standard Martley green and chocolate, with black and white lining. On the maker's photograph at least, lining had normal corners rather than being incurved. The new numberplate was placed centrally on the tanksides, with a narrow band of black and white lining around its perimeter. The main tankside lining was formed into two panels, the inner verticals skirting around the numberplate.

From the arrival of Mr Kirtley's 'B' Class 0-6-0 goods engines of 1876, a more noticeable change was apparent. The 'B' Class arrived in glossy black, lined with slate grey bands, fine-lined on each side with vermilion. It is possible that this was seen as a goods-only livery, and the original specification for Mr Kirtley's next design, the 'M' Class 4-4-0s of 1877, was for them to be painted green. However, these were all actually delivered in black, and shortly afterwards black was introduced for all Kirtley engines.

A paint specification of 1890 determined that locomotives were to receive one coat of lead colour, stopping and filling, another coat of lead colour, then two coats of drop black, followed by one coat of

341
London Chatham & Dover Railway

'Little Scotchman' Class 0-4-2 No. 89, formerly *Kelvin*, was built by Neilson & Co of Glasgow in 1866 to a design by Mr Martley. It was rebuilt at Longhenge works in 1880.
Author's collection

Disposition of lettering and device on First class carriages. Second class had the script "LC&DR" instead.

London Chatham & Dover Railway

black japan. Lining of slate grey bands fine-lined with a vermilion outer line and a yellow inner was then applied, followed by four coats of best copal varnish. The original form of the grey body lining used incurved corners, but from 1892 the more conventional convex corners were applied. Frames, boiler bands and wheels were lined with vermilion only. Axles, motion and inside faces of the frames were finished in vermilion. The inside of the cab was 'purple brown'.

Bufferbeams were vermilion, edged with a black line, and buffer casings were also black. The number was applied in the form "Nº [hook] 12" in 10-inch seriffed gold characters shaded with black to the right and below. The small "o" was underlined with a dash, and below that a square full stop.

The standard numberplate was fixed to the cab sides or the centre of tanks. The only other sign of ownership appeared on tenders. This was an ornate rendering in gold script of the company initials "LC&DR", shaded in red. A small maker's plate was also usually evident, on a driving wheel splasher or on the bunkers of tank engines. Many of Mr Martley's engines had a maker's plate on the outside frames below the platform.

Goods engines were also black, and although they followed the same general arrangement as passenger engines, including the decorative script "LC&DR" on tenders, they were lined in panels of parallel vermilion lines only.

Meanwhile, although Martley engines remained in green, there was a subtle change in their lining, possibly to maintain a familial resemblance to the black engines. Panels were edged in black, now fine-lined vermilion. The inner black lining was still fine-lined on the inside with white, but the outside was now fine-lined with vermilion. Boiler bands were black edged in vermilion, with a white line on the boiler clothing about 1 inch away on each side. When receiving minor attention at Longhedge, cabs and the Westinghouse brake were supplied, and obsolete features were removed, but the green livery was retained. It was not until the Martley engines were completely rebuilt that they were outshopped in black, their names removed and standard numberplates fixed on their cabsides or bunkers. The 'Europa' Class 2-4-0s were among the last to be rebuilt in 1892.

The carriages of the LC&DR were built of teak and were oil-lit, and remained so until the merger with the SER. Only a handful

London Chatham & Dover Railway

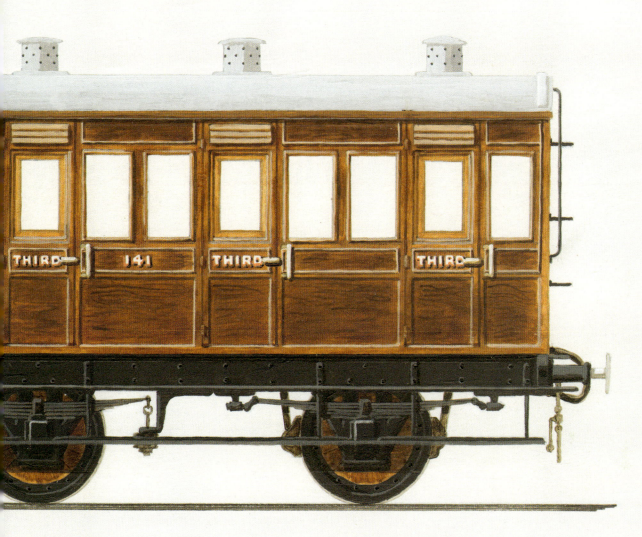

of examples were converted to electric lighting in the last years of the separate company. The Westinghouse brake was provided from about 1887.

The original carriages were all 4-wheeled and very standardised, being 25 feet in length, increasing to 26 feet from 1880. Body panels, quarter lights and fascia had right-angled corners, a feature that persisted on all the carriages of the company. Six-wheeled carriages appeared from 1885, being 28 feet or 30 feet in length. Bogie carriages also appeared in 1885, with the 40-foot First/Second Composites of the 'Boat Train Stock', but the LC&DR could not afford to build more bogie carriages until 1894 and 1897, and as a result had a very low proportion of them (less than 10%) in its stock at the 1899 merger. The newer bogie vehicles were up to 46 feet long.

Carriages were varnished teak without lining throughout the life of the company. Solebars were almost certainly originally painted 'teak colour', as specified by Mr Kirtley in 1885 for the carriages of the Hull & Barnsley Railway to whom he was acting as consultant (see Volume 2). Roofs were apparently not white, but a light lead grey when new. Below the solebar, underframe details were black.

Wheel centres were also painted teak colour. With the widespread use of steel underfames, as on the bogie stock, solebars were painted black, as were bogies.

Some non-passenger carriage vehicles (horseboxes for example) are believed to have been varnished teak, but those vehicles not built of teak are known to have been painted 'brown' (teak colour), at least by 1898.

Lettering was in gold sans-serif characters. *Moore's Monthly Magazine* in 1896 gives the shading colour as red, and surviving remains confirm this. Unusually, the red shading is to the right of each character, combined with the black below, rather than black being a separate 'shadow' as was usual practice.

Class marking was in words "FIRST", "SECOND" or "THIRD" on the waist panels of compartment doors. Brake compartments featured "LUGGAGE" and "GUARD" on the double doors. The disposition of the remaining markings depended on the class of vehicle.

First class and First/Second Composites carried the ornate armorial device on the bottom quarter panels. This consisted of the motto "INVICTA" surrounded by four coats of arms: Kent with its

344
London Chatham & Dover Railway

white horse at the top, London to the left, Dover to the right, and Rochester below. The whole was encircled by a garter carrying the name of the company. There were two on each side, with running numbers above in the waist panel. Bogie vehicles had this between the outer compartments, roughly above the bogie centres.

Second class had a similar arrangement, except a gilt monogram of the letters "LC&DR" was used instead of the device. These monograms were the same design as those on the locomotives, but shaded only in black. There were two per side, even on 4- and 6-wheeled vehicles, with the numbers in the waist panels above.

Third class vehicles had neither monogram nor device, and were lettered with "LC&DR" and the number in the waist. The bogie Thirds once again had initials and numbers in pairs between the outer compartments, over the bogie centres.

The wagons of the LC&DR, compared to other contemporary railways, had a rather archaic appearance. Many of the open wagons had high curved ends to support wagon sheets and the vans had vertical outside framing. The goods brakes also had outside framing and were, except for some end windows, almost totally enclosed. They were provided with a goods compartment with double doors to take tariffs.

Wagons were painted a light medium lead grey, with black below the solebar. Lettering from at least the 1870s was in small, white sans-serif characters, being only about 6 inches high. The company markings eschewed the use of the ampersand, and the initials "L C D R" were widely-spaced along the body. Three-plank opens had the initials on the middle plank, but higher-sided wagons and vans had them on the second plank down from the top. Brakes were lettered five planks down from the top, proportionally about two thirds of the body side up from the bottom rail.

Numbers were painted in the same size characters to lower right, and to lower left was painted in script "To Carry" followed by the allowed load in tons, hundredweights and quarters.

Wagon sheets carried the initials (probably just "LCDR" like the wagons) and the number, but are reported not to have had any other distinguishing marks.

1 'Martley Green' Carter 15 Pantone 7483C BS 381C 226 'Mid Brunswick Green'	2 'Martley Chocolate' Carter 38 Pantone 4625C BS 381C 412 'Dark Brown'	3 'Vermilion' Carter 36 Pantone 485C BS 4800 04 E 53 'Poppy Red'

London Tilbury & Southend Railway

The London Tilbury & Southend Railway was promoted jointly by the Eastern Counties and the London & Blackwall railways in 1852. The line was opened to Tilbury in 1854, and Southend in 1855, worked under lease by the contractors Peto, Brassey & Betts. Trains ran from Bishopsgate and Fenchurch Street until an avoiding line was opened to Barking in 1858, then services ran from Fenchurch Street only. The railway was reconstituted as an independent company in 1862 but was still under lease until 1875, at which time the Great Eastern Railway supplied rolling stock until the LT&SR had enough carriages and locomotives of their own. A works was established at Plaistow, and Mr Thomas Whitelegg was installed as Locomotive Superintendent where he stayed until succeeded by his son Robert in 1910.

The LT&SR expanded; to Shoeburyness (1884), to Southend via Upminster (1888), and to Romford (1892). Joint lines included the 1894 Tottenham & Forest Gate Railway with the Midland, which allowed the LT&SR to run into St. Pancras, and the 1902 Whitechapel & Bow Railway with the District Railway. The LT&SR owned 79 miles of line, and six river steamers for the ferry service from Tilbury to Gravesend.

The Midland Railway absorbed the LT&SR in 1912. Consequently, the LT&SR became part of the London Midland & Scottish Railway in 1923 and passed into the London Midland Region of British Railways in 1948. However, in 1949 the former LT&SR was reallocated to the Eastern Region.

The LT&SR was considered by the *Locomotive Magazine* of 1897 to have the most gaudily-painted engines running into London. The main body colour was a bright green [1], applied to boilers, body panels and outside cylinders. This colour was edged with a broad purple brown [2] border, fine-lined vermilion. Those engines with 'wrap-over' cabs had this edging taken over the green roof to the other side. Tanks, bunkers and cylinders were lined with a black band, fine-lined in white. Boiler bands were purple brown, fine-lined on each edge in vermilion, with a black band on the boiler on each side, lined on the outer edge with white. Cab interiors were painted purple brown, and ordinary roofs were black.

The Westinghouse brake pump cylinders were painted green even if mounted on the smokebox, with polished cylinder covers, and lined out in the compressed style used on the splashers of the 1903 '69' Class 0-6-2Ts, having purple brown, vermilion, black and white next to each other.

Below the footplate, valances, steps, frames and splashers were purple brown, edged with black before being fine-lined with vermilion. In addition, splashers, valances and steps had an inner line of yellow. Wheels were green, with purple brown tyres and edges to the bosses. The inner edges of the purple brown were lined with vermilion. Axle ends were black lined in white.

Bufferbeams were vermilion edged in black, fine-lined yellow. There was more lining around the slot accommodating the drawhook, and around the outer end of the buffer casing. Engine numbers were placed in the upper part of the bufferbeam in the form "Nº 31" for example, in gold seriffed characters shaded in black. Guard irons were vermilion.

All tank engines were identified by names, executed in gold serif characters shaded in black, arching over a central armorial device. The only engines to carry initials were the two '49' Class 0-6-0s, which had "L. T. & S. R." in sans-serif gold characters on their tenders, and the device on their cab side sheets, although they

Tilbury Docks, from the Railway Magazine (March 1902). Author's collection

London Tilbury & Southend Railway

were delivered in a slightly different style. The device featured the gatehouse of Tilbury Fort within a blue garter, flanked by the arms of London, Essex and Kent.

Four engines were fitted with condensing apparatus for use on the new Whitechapel & Bow line. On these engines ('No. 1' Class numbers 3, 7, 23 and 29), the green was replaced by black japan, but the purple brown areas remained as before. Cab interiors were reportedly light blue.

From about 1906 more changes began to become apparent. The remaining 'No. 1' Class 4-4-2Ts and the two 0-6-0s had their black and white lining omitted on repainting. The second group of '69' Class 0-6-2Ts were delivered in this state, the 1903 examples eventually being repainted accordingly. Another small change which I consider dates from this time was the painting of buffer casings purple brown instead of vermilion. The outer end of the casing was lined in black, vermilion and yellow. The black and yellow edging on the bufferbeam was now taken round the base of each buffer as well.

Perhaps more noticeably, the '37' Class 4-4-2Ts rebuilt in the period up to 1909 (numbers 37, 38, 39, 43 and 47), and the first two '79' Class 4-4-2Ts of 1909 (numbers 79 and 80) appeared in traffic painted grey [3], with all lining in black and white. Various commentators have called this 'lavender', but in my opinion it was merely varnished paintshop lead grey. Engine No. 80 in the temporary guise of *Southend-on-Sea* was shown in this form at the International Exhibition, and won a medal. The grey engines were all repainted green by 1910.

There were other differences on all the rebuilt '37' Class engines and the similar '79' Class. Safety valves were enclosed in a brass casing, but only No. 80, now named *Thundersley*, had it polished. The latter engine also carried a facsimile of its exhibition medal on the tank below the name and above the device. The device itself was mounted on a circular brass plaque on all these engines. There was more polished metal in the form of a brass lip to the chimney flare, a brass lip to the bases of the dome and safety valve cover (also lined in black and white), and polished steel cylinder covers. Cylinder wrappers were not painted but were blued steel. Wheel tyres had the outer ½ inch of the steel free of paint and polished.

Under Robert Whitelegg, names became gilt transfers with shading in blue, and on bufferbeams "Nº" was dropped and the numerals placed centrally, over the drawhook.

On the acquisition of the LT&SR by the Midland in 1912, the standard MR crimson [4] with simple lining and tankside numbers was applied to most engines, except the 0-6-2Ts and the 0-6-0s, which were unlined black. Mr Whitelegg's new class of 4-6-4T locomotives, and a further group of 0-6-2Ts which were all delivered in 1912, were treated as Midland engines and never carried LT&SR livery.

347
London Tilbury & Southend Railway

Forest Gate, from the Railway Magazine (January 1910). Author's collection

348
London Tilbury & Southend Railway

LT&SR 0-6-0 No. 49, one of a pair delivered in 1898 that had been built for the Ottoman Railway. *Author's collection*

349
London Tilbury & Southend Railway

Carriages were varnished teak without lining. Roofs were white, solebars were 'teak' brown, and ironwork below the solebar and steps and handrails on carriage ends were black. Wheel tyres were white. Brake ends were painted vermilion.

Lettering was in gold sans serif characters, 3 inches high, shaded to the left in red and white, and shadowed to the right in black. In the earlier period class marking was in words, but after the introduction of bogie stock in 1901 class marking became large seriffed numerals on the lower door panels. Smoking compartments then had "SMOKING" on the door waist panel, and also blue "SMOKING" stickers on the windows. The standard arrangement for initials and number was to have "L.T. & S.R." twice on the carriage side, with the number central, preceded by "Nº", although some vehicles did not allow a symmetrical layout. The device was placed twice per side on bogie stock, but once on other stock, always under either the number or the initials.

LT&SR bogie Brake Third No. 50. Author's collection

350
London Tilbury & Southend Railway

New stock for the Ealing to Southend service was delivered in 1912. The class, initials and number were all in 6-inch brass characters fixed to the waist panels, for example "FIRST CLASS LT&SR Nº 47 THIRD CLASS". First class had the white numeral "1" displayed on the window glass.

The Midland repainted carriage stock only slowly, and for several years teak stock could be seen carrying the word "MIDLAND" in gilt transfers on a black rectangle in the eaves panel.

Non-passenger vehicles such as horseboxes, carriage trucks and milk vans were painted a 'teak' colour and lettered in similar transfers to the passenger stock. Horseboxes actually carried the device below the lettering, which was arranged centrally on the dropping part of the door.

Goods stock was painted a light grey, with black below the solebar. Lettering was pale yellow, although a few grey examples had black letters. The earlier lettering was "L.T & S.R" about 6 inches high shaded in black, placed on the lower left, with the number in the corresponding position on the right. By 1904 size had been increased to a maximum of about 14 inches and shading omitted. If no frame members intruded, square full stops were used, and the central ampersand was only about 7 inches high. Numbers were usually in small numerals to the right, but brake vans had them centrally on the bottom plank. Exceptions to the light grey were gunpowder vans, which were vermilion, and some fish vans, which may have been light green or blue, lettered in black.

From circa 1900 a cast iron numberplate was used. This was rectangular with concave corners similar to the Midland design. The lettering was white on a black background, having "LONDON TILBURY" above and "& SOUTHEND RY" below the central number, which was preceded by "Nº".

Wagon sheets are reported to have had the usual initials, but were further distinguished by one blue diagonal stripe from corner to corner.

Metropolitan District Railway

The Metropolitan District Railway, usually known simply as the 'District', was incorporated in 1864. It was originally intended as a subsidiary of the Metropolitan Railway, as a means to complete the underground Inner Circle already begun, and would have been formally amalgamated with that concern in due time. The railway was built mostly using the cut-and-cover method under public highways. The first section from South Kensington to Westminster was opened on Christmas Eve 1868 and worked by the Metropolitan. An extension westwards to West Brompton (alongside the West London Extension Railway's station) was opened in 1869, and eastwards the work was opened in stages under the new Victoria Embankment until it reached Mansion House in 1871.

Meanwhile, many Directors of the railway were dissatisfied with the Metropolitan's working of the services, and their agreement was terminated on 3rd July 1871, the day of the Mansion House opening. On that day, new locomotives and stock built specifically for the District Railway began working their own trains. Relations between the two railways deteriorated. Coupled with a severe lack of capital, this ensured that the completion of the Inner Circle was delayed for several years, finally being achieved by a joint railway in October 1884.

In the west of the system, the District extended into the open air at Earl's Court to a north-facing junction with the West London Extension Railway at Kensington (Addison Road), and from there District trains began running to Richmond over the London & South Western Railway's branch in 1877. A branch to Ealing Broadway followed two years later. Next was an extension southwards to Putney Bridge in 1880 from the old West Brompton terminus. Having acquired a taste for expansion into the western suburbs, the District opened a branch to Hounslow Town in 1883, extended to Hounslow Barracks in 1884. The Putney Bridge line was extended by the L&SWR to Wimbledon in 1889, District services beginning over it forthwith. The last western development was the building of the Ealing to South Harrow line, finished in 1899, but not opened.

In the east, the Whitechapel & Bow Railway opened in 1902 as a joint railway between the District and the London Tilbury & Southend Railway, allowing through trains to East Ham and Upminster.

District Railway No. 20, one of the original twenty-four locomotives built by Beyer, Peacock in 1871. Author's collection

352
Metropolitan District Railway

Meanwhile, new deep-level 'tube' railways were opened by the City & South London Railway in 1890, the Waterloo & City in 1898 and the Central London Railway or 'Tuppeny Tube' in 1900. They began syphoning off passengers from both the Metropolitan and the District railways with their cleanliness and simple fare structures. The steam underground railways were seen as becoming obsolete. Grimy, hot, smoky and uncomfortable; electrification was the obvious solution.

An experiment was undertaken jointly by the Metropolitan and District railways on the short spur from Earl's Court to Kensington High Street, opened to the public in June 1900. After this rather pointless exercise, the two railways made a joint consultation and (unaccountably) decided to electrify on the Ganz overhead wire three-phase alternating current system.

The District found it almost impossible to find capital investment for the electrification project, and had to look to the American financier and railway promoter Charles Yerkes. He acquired a controlling interest in the District Railway and several other proposed London tube railways during 1901, and with a new Chairman of the District, Robert (later Sir Robert) Perks MP, undertook the task with an urgency that both astonished and gratified the *Railway Magazine*, for whom electrification could not come soon enough.

Mr Yerkes and his technical advisor James Russell Chapman understandably disagreed strongly with the Ganz system, and favoured the live rail direct current system they had already used in America. Only after arbitration by the Board of Trade was the DC method of traction adopted for the whole network, using a four-rail system.

Mr Yerkes established the Metropolitan District Electric Traction Company to carry out the electrification work and created the Underground Electric Railways Company of London (UERL) to manage the District Railway and his many tube railways then under construction.

An electric service on the 1899 Ealing to South Harrow line was introduced in 1903 and was used to test equipment and instruct crews before full electrification. Electric working began on the Hounslow Branch on 13th June 1905, followed by District services

353 Metropolitan District Railway

from Ealing to Whitechapel on 1st July. This was also intended to be the first day of full electric working on the Inner Circle, but a mishap delayed that until 24th September. The last District public steam trains ran on Sunday 5th November 1905.

The District opened its own engineering works in 1871 at Lillie Bridge, just west of Earl's Court station, off Lillie Road. On electrification, the District opened a new Works at Mill Hill Park, later known as Ealing Common.

In 1908, the co-operation that had already ensued between the railways owned by Yerkes's UERL became manifest with a formal agreement, generating a new map and signage depicting the whole group as the "UNDERGROUND". Eventually the District, along with the Metropolitan, the Hammersmith & City and the deep tube railways, all became part of the London Passenger Transport Board (known as London Transport) in 1933.

The steam locomotives delivered to the District from Beyer, Peacock in 1871 were 4-4-0 'condensing' tank engines very similar to those of the Metropolitan Railway, including their colour, described as a dark blue-green, or a 'bright' green. The lining style was very different; Metropolitan engines had their tanks built up from three plates, lined out in three panels, but District engines had smooth-sided tanks lined in a single panel. The lining seems to have been black, fine-lined on the outer edge with vermilion [1], and on the inner edge with white. Corners were at first rounded. It is said that in order to distinguish the engines of one railway from another for the passengers, the District used the letters A to X to identify each of the first twenty-four delivered, rather than numbers. There was no other identification, the tankside carrying only a central Beyer, Peacock plate.

When the next batch of engines was delivered in 1876, numbers were adopted, their position being on the bufferbeam in the conventional style, for example "Nº [hook] 4". Under the "o" was not only a dash but a dot as well. Bufferbeams appear to have been plain vermilion. Further batches of engines were delivered between 1881 and 1886, bringing the total up to fifty-four. Tenders were sought for a further batch of locomotives in 1900, won by Dübs & Co. of Glasgow, but after the decision to electrify had been made, this contract was cancelled.

Metropolitan District Railway

By 1883, lettering had been adopted on the tanks, consisting of "DISTRICT [plate] RAILWAY" on either side of the builders plate. Characters were plain sans-serif in white, shaded in black, with the initial letters of the words slightly larger than the rest. The engine number was placed above the plate. Also by this time, the lining had square corners. Shortly after this, the livery of the locomotives was altered.

The new colour was a darker, more 'olive' green. Body panels were edged in black, with a fine vermilion line between the black and the green. Tanks and bunkers were lined in black with square corners, fine-lined with vermilion. Boiler bands were also black, fine-lined vermilion. This livery was enlivened by the polished brass dome, the brass fillet between boiler and smokebox, and much more polished brass and copper, such as the copper cap to the combined tank vent. Bufferbeams were vermilion, with the number applied as usual, and the tank lettering was retained unaltered from the earlier livery. Wheels were olive green, with black tyres and axle ends, both of which were fine-lined in vermilion.

On electrification all but six of the locomotives were withdrawn, and four of these went in 1909, leaving just numbers 33 and 34 which acted as short trip and shunting engines at the old Lillie Bridge Works. The livery of this final period remained dark olive green, but the lining was simplified to a black edge around the tanks and bunkers, fine-lined in vermilion. Wheels remained green with black tyres and axle ends fine-lined in vermilion. The engines were withdrawn in 1926 and 1932 respectively.

Until electrification, all District carriages were four-wheeled and 26ft 6ins long over the body. The body styling was very similar to the contemporary Metropolitan carriages, with rounded tops to the doors to bring them within the structure gauge if opened

355
Metropolitan District Railway

accidentally. First class carriages had four compartments, but Second and Third had five. Wheels were 3ft 6in diameter and open-spoke.

The carriages were close-coupled into nineteen sets of eight vehicles, the carriages at each end being Brake vehicles. Four more trains were acquired in 1879, and these and all subsequent sets were nine-carriage. Subsequent batches of vehicles (twenty sets between 1880 and 1891) had a variety of slightly different stylings, but were essentially the same as the first ones ordered.

Originally, carriages were fitted with a roof structure that looked like a clerestory, but in fact contained the rubber gas bag to supply the roof lamps. Late in 1880, an agreement was made with Pintsch's Patent Lighting Co. for the supply of the more normal compressed gas fittings, and these 'clerestories' were removed.

The roofs of many sets used on the Inner Circle services were fitted in 1894 with large ventilator-shaped boxes. These contained the workings of a crude indicator system, supplied by The Indicator Company, notifying passengers of the next stop. When not working correctly some very misleading indications could be given, and within a few years the system was abandoned, although the boxes persisted.

Carriages were panelled in teak, and when new were merely varnished. After a period of time, a painted finish was applied, described both as 'dark brown' and 'red-chocolate', no doubt meant to be a substitute for the original wood colour. Brake ends were painted vermilion. Roofs were white when new, but exposure to the London atmosphere and the miasma through the tunnels rapidly turned this to grey and then black.

Lettering was in gold, shaded with blue and shadowed in black. Doors carried the class in full, for example "SECOND CLASS" on two lines. The name of the company was central on the waist,

356
Metropolitan District Railway

Metropolitan District condensing locomotive No. 4 heads a 9-coach Wimbledon train.   Author's collection

Third class 4-wheeled carriage No. 85.   Author's collection

originally being "METROPOLITAN [door] DISTRICT". By the 1890s the company name had been simplified to "DISTRICT [door] RAILWAY", and class marking was in large numerals on the waist of the door. Vehicle numbers were placed two to each side beyond the lettering throughout all periods.

Six sets of new carriages were ordered in 1900 for the Whitechapel & Bow Railway; they were to be considered 'joint' stock, although three sets were allocated to the LT&SR, and three to the District.

They were once again built in teak and had four wheels, being 26ft 4¾ins over the bodies. The nine-car sets were marshalled: Bk.2nd/2nd/2nd/2nd/1st/1st/3rd/3rd/3rd/Bk.3rd. This had probably been the standard for all District trains since 1879.

Upon electrification, the District's old steam-hauled carriages were sold off, as were three of the experimental set of six electric vehicles run on the Earl's Court to Kensington High Street line, which were sold to the Colne Valley & Halstead Railway in 1906.

Metropolitan District Railway

Steel bodied electric locomotive No. 7A heads a rake of LM&SR 4- and 6-wheeled stock in 1925. Note the revised position of the number below the open cab window, the "UNDERGROUND" under the second window, and the grey doors and roof strip of this era.
Author's collection

The first electric train on the District Railway. *Author's collection*

The original vehicles used on the South Harrow line in 1903 were entirely American in outline. Each 'car' was built of timber, flat-sided, with a clerestory roof having dressed-off ends, rows of small arch-topped windows, and central sliding doors. Apart from the driving motor cars, which had enclosed cabs and a luggage compartment, each end had a gated open verandah. Several years later, these cars became known as the 'A' Stock. They were meant to run in seven-car formations, but rarely did so.

In 1903, the District ordered sixty more seven-car sets of electric stock, which would replace all the original steam-hauled carriages upon complete electrification in 1905. They were later known as the 'B Stock'. The cars were again to the American pattern, but gone were the verandahs, which were drafty and unpopular. The open seating area was provided with large, square windows, each having a slightly curved transom under the toplights. There were three sliding doors on each side of a trailer car, and the driving cars

358
Metropolitan District Railway

again had a cab and a luggage area. The luggage areas were removed in favour of First class seating in 1910.

The District also purchased ten electric locomotives, numbered 1A to 10A, delivered in 1905 and ready for traffic by December of that year. They were originally single-ended and ran coupled together in pairs, cabs outermost. Their bodywork was similar to that of the multiple units (although built of steel), but at 25ft 10½ins they were much shorter.

The locomotives were used on the Broad Street to Mansion House 'Outer Circle' route, attached and detached at Earl's Court. When this service ceased at the beginning of 1909, the locomotives hauled regular District 'Inner Circle' trains until a through Ealing to Southend service was inaugurated with the London Tilbury & Southend Railway from 1st June 1910, the District electric locomotives being substituted for the LT&SR steam locomotives at Barking.

The District were experimenting with liveries on the 'A Stock'. The first colour chosen was yellow, lined in 'maroon', but shortly afterwards two sets of four cars were running in a variety of colours. One set had the driving cars at each end in yellow (possibly lemon chrome), but the two central trailer cars were painted with dark red lower panels, and white above the waist. The other set noted had one driving unit in the dark red and white, but the remaining three cars in 'brilliant' red.

That word was well-applied, for the colour finally chosen for all District electric stock was vermilion, described in the *Locomotive Magazine* as 'bright red' and 'light red', and in the *Railway Magazine* as 'brilliant red' and 'scarlet'. The wooden sliding doors and the window frames remained in natural varnished teak. The bottom panels were separated into two by the central doors, and were lined at top and sides only, possibly in gold, with a decorative detail in each corner. Roofs were lead grey.

The long eaves panels of both electric multiple units and locomotives were lettered "DISTRICT RAILWAY" in gold seriffed characters, continuing the American theme. The blank panel of the luggage area was lettered with "LUGGAGE / COMPARTMENT" on two lines, the upper word "LUGGAGE" being arranged in an arc. The vehicle number was placed centrally on each of the lower side panels, again in a seriffed style. The electric locomotives had their numbers preceded by "Nº". Lettering was apparently shaded

359
Metropolitan District Railway

A two-car train of Class 'A' stock at Acton Town, 10th May 1925.

Author's collection

Metropolitan District Railway

Three-car train of 'F Stock' at Acton Town, 10th May 1925. *Author's collection*

with blue and white. It is not known how long this original form of lettering survived, but there is reason to suppose from photographs until at least 1909.

The vermilion livery was not universally appreciated, and it was reportedly difficult to keep the wooden bodies clean. From the beginning of 1907, a Brunswick green livery was substituted, which the *Railway Magazine* found more to its taste, calling it 'neater'. However, by November of that year, the livery had reverted to vermilion, and it is thought that, at most, only half of the rolling stock had been repainted during that time.

Upon the pooling agreement between members of the UERL group in 1908, a new lettering style of "Underground" soon appeared on signage. All that happened on the rolling stock was the gradual omission of the "DISTRICT RAILWAY" branding, leaving only two running numbers on the lower body of each car, arranged symmetrically on each side of the central doors.

In 1911 more stock was delivered, very similar to the 'B Stock', but with steel body parts and no luggage areas. The windows had straight transoms under the toplights. This was the 'C Stock', followed by the identical 'D Stock' in 1912. The 'E Stock' of 1914 differed only in an elliptical roof replacing the old clerestory design. All of this stock was painted vermilion without branding or lining, just two running numbers on each side. There are also suggestions by this date that the top strip above the windows, and a band along the bottom of the body were painted 'chocolate', but I can find no further information.

After the First World War, all-steel stock to a new design was ordered, delivered in 1920 and 1921. The bodies of this stock, later known as the 'F Stock' (and nick-named 'The Tanks'), were completely different, with contoured sides, fewer windows, elliptical roofs and a pair of large oval windows in each end. Their livery was different too. Gone was the vermilion, replaced by a deeper shade of red, referred to as 'engine lake'. This was a brownish crimson, apparently very similar to the livery of the steam locomotives of the Metropolitan Railway. When delivered, each car had only one number on each side, in the lower left-hand panel, and no branding.

The rest of the rolling stock was repainted to match, with one difference. From about 1921 it was specified that the wooden doors and window frames, including the clerestories of the older stock, were to be painted grey. The strip along the top of each side at cornice level was also so treated. Photographs show a light medium grey. The electric locomotives lost the "Nº" preceding their running number.

From 1923 lettering also changed, there now being the word "UNDERGROUND" on the lower bodies, in the new corporate sans-serif style, with two running numbers towards each end, frequently still in the seriffed style. The "UNDERGROUND" branding was as near as possible central, but because nearly all stock had central doors, it was placed just to the right.

The District did not possess any goods stock as such, and goods traffic did not form any part of its own working, but goods stations belonging to the Midland railway occurred at Kensington and Brompton. There were a few wagons for internal use, twenty-seven in 1888; these were apparently marked "D R" and were probably grey, but little information about them exists.

1   'Vermilion'
Carter 36
Pantone 485C
BS 4800 04 E 53
'Poppy Red'

Metropolitan Railway

The world's first underground railway was incorporated as the North Metropolitan Railway in 1853, for a line from the Great Western Railway's Paddington terminus into the City of London. The name was changed to the Metropolitan Railway in the following year, with permission to connect with the Great Northern Railway at their King's Cross terminus. Construction started in 1859, mostly using the 'cut-and-cover' method under existing streets, now termed a 'sub-surface' railway.

The Metropolitan Railway opened in January 1863, the mixed-gauge line running from Paddington (Bishop's Road) in the west to Farringdon Street near Smithfield Market in the east. Initially the trains were provided by the GWR (using their broad gauge rolling stock), but a disagreement prompted the withdrawal of their trains in August 1863. The Metropolitan ordered locomotives and rolling stock of its own, and until they arrived in 1864, the train service was run using GNR stock. The GWR resumed services in October 1863.

An extension westwards, the Hammersmith & City Railway, was opened in 1864 from Paddington (Bishop's Road) to Hammersmith, with a spur to the West London Railway at Kensington (Addison Road). It was again mixed gauge to allow GWR broad gauge trains to run over the line, which became joint Metropolitan and GWR property in 1867. The broad gauge rail was eventually removed from all the Metropolitan and Hammersmith & City lines in 1869.

An extension eastwards to Moorgate was opened in 1865. A standard gauge parallel route was built at the same time from connecting tunnels with the Midland Railway at St. Pancras and the GNR connecting tunnels at King's Cross, opened in 1868 and known as the City Widened Lines. Connections ran south from here through the Snow Hill tunnel to the London Chatham & Dover Railway at Blackfriars. The MR, GNR and the GWR all opened goods stations off the Widened Lines, and the Metropolitan had its own goods sidings at Moorgate.

The Metropolitan proposed to extend its line to South Kensington, but there were now many other conflicting proposals for underground railways in London. A Parliamentary Joint Committee of 1864 recommended that the best course would be to make a circular railway, the southern part to be completed by the Metropolitan District Railway. The 'District' was incorporated as a separate concern to allow independent financing, but was at this stage very much a subsidiary of the Metropolitan (see previous chapter).

The Metropolitan's extension left the original line at Praed Street Junction near Paddington, and opened to South Kensington in 1868, at the same time as the District's line from South Kensington

No. 103, from the *Railway Magazine* (September 1922).   Author's collection

Metropolitan Railway

Beyer, Peacock condensing 4-4-0T No. 27. *Author's collection*

to Westminster. The District extended eastwards to Mansion House and the Metropolitan extended eastwards to Aldgate in 1876, but the circuit was not fully completed until 1884, achieved by a joint District and Metropolitan railway.

The Metropolitan & St. John's Wood Railway was a single line from Baker Street to Swiss Cottage, opened in 1868 and worked by the Metropolitan. The new Chairman, Sir Edward Watkin, saw it as essential to escape the confinement of London which was so hampering the fortunes of the District Railway, and used the branch as a basis for extension into the Middlesex and Buckinghamshire countryside to generate more traffic, in particular goods traffic. The first section of the line, which emerged into the open air at Finchley Road (where there was a goods transfer line from the MR), was opened to Willesden Green in 1879, then to Harrow-on-the-Hill in 1880. The St. John's Wood Railway was absorbed by the Metropolitan in 1882, and the original line doubled.

A further extension from Harrow was authorised to join the existing Aylesbury & Buckingham Railway (1868), which ran from Aylesbury to Quainton Road, and then to Verney Junction on the London & North Western Railway's Oxford line. The Metropolitan Railway's extension opened to Rickmansworth in 1887, Chesham in 1889, and finally Aylesbury in 1892. The A&BR was absorbed and upgraded to main line standards. Trains started running from Baker Street to Verney Junction in 1897.

Another local line, the Oxford & Aylesbury Tramway or 'Brill Branch', left the main line at Quainton Road and was worked by the Metropolitan from 1899.

Sir Edward Watkin was also Chairman of the Manchester Sheffield & Lincolnshire Railway (renamed the Great Central Railway in 1897) and had masterminded their London extension, which reached Quainton Road in 1898. The GCR had running powers over the Metropolitan to Harrow, and then separate lines to its terminus at Marylebone, opened in 1899. The shared lines, including the branch to Chesham and the Brill Branch, became the Metropolitan & Great Central Joint Railway in 1906.

Meanwhile, the new deep-level 'tube' railways were attracting passengers away from the smoky atmosphere of both the District and the Metropolitan railways. Electrification was seen as the only way forward. The story of electrification was covered more fully in the previous chapter. Suffice it here to say that the Inner Circle was electrified by 24th September 1905, followed by the Hammersmith & City line in December 1906, but, unlike the District, not all the Metropolitan was converted.

The Metropolitan was different in that a large proportion of its line consisted of ordinary stations in the countryside far away from the urban sprawl of London, which called for a combined electric and steam approach. The electrification was opened to the terminus at Uxbridge on 1st January 1905, but services from Baker Street to Aylesbury and beyond were still steam hauled throughout. After the arrival of some electric locomotives, the changeover to steam traction occurred from 1st November 1906 at Wembley Park. The electrified section was extended to Harrow, and steam locomotives replaced the electric locomotives there from 19th July 1908, the reverse happening on the return journey.

Metropolitan Railway

Metropolitan Railway 0-4-4T condensing engine No. 68.　　　　　　　　　　Author's collection

In 1908, the Metropolitan joined the co-operative agreement formed between the railways owned by the Underground Electric Railways Company of London, which generated a new map and signage in London depicting the whole group as the 'UNDERGROUND'. The Metropolitan resisted any move towards closer amalgamation, pointing out that it was unique among the Underground railways in that it had connections with main line overground railways and had a thriving freight business.

Electrification was eventually extended to Rickmansworth on 5th January 1925. The Metropolitan continued to open new lines, to Watford (1925) and Stanmore (1932), but it was the promotion of the countryside along the main line and the new houses being built there as 'Metro-land' that made the Metropolitan a household name.

The Metropolitan was not included in the Grouping of the Railways Act, and remained stubbornly independent, opposing the London Passenger Transport Bill of 1931, but nevertheless becoming part of the London Passenger Transport Board in 1933. The Metropolitan steam services, and most of the locomotives, were made over to the London & North Eastern Railway in 1937. The Metropolitan & Great Central Joint Railway maintained its legal existence until Nationalisation in 1948, when it became part of British Railways (Eastern Region) until the ex-GCR London Extension was transferred to the London Midland Region in 1958.

The original engineering works of the Metropolitan Railway were at Edgware Road station, adjoining Chapel Road, but in 1882 the Works were moved to a new site at Neasden, where their power station for electrification was also built in 1904. Locomotive Superintendents in the modern era were Mr J.J. Hanbury (1885-96), Mr T.F. Clarke (1896-1903) and Mr Charles Jones (1903-33), termed Chief Electrical and Locomotive Engineer from 1917.

The Met's first locomotives, the Beyer, Peacock 4-4-0Ts, were painted green, with brass domes and copper chimney caps. Lining was present, but details are uncertain. Buffer beams were red, and the number appeared in brass numerals on the chimney front. The first eighteen locomotives were named, the brass nameplate being mounted on the boiler.

From 1885 the locomotive colour changed to a deep crimson, similar to the Midland Railway colour. The heavily-rivetted tanks of the 4-4-0Ts were covered with plain sheets in three sections to facilitate lettering and lining. Lining was in black, the tanksides divided into three panels following the joints of the sheeting. Fine-lining and lettering was in 'straw', probably lemon chrome. Domes were polished brass, with brass numerals on chimneys, and nameplates were removed. Wheel tyres were black, and the wheel bosses were lined in black and yellow. Buffer beams were vermilion, serif numerals being painted on the rear one in the usual form, for example "Nº [hook] 58", probably in gold, shaded in black.

The middle panel of the sidetanks featured a large painted number, surrounded by two ellipses creating a border, which contained "METROPOLITAN" above and "RAILWAY." below, all in lemon chrome seriffed characters shaded to left and below in black.

The Class 'C' 0-4-4Ts of 1891 (originally designed by James Stirling for the South Eastern Railway) deviated from the usual

364
Metropolitan Railway

standard by having their smooth-sided tanks lined out in a single panel, as depicted on the painting, but they retained the large painted number and surrounding lettering.

Mr Clark introduced similar but larger locomotives, the Class 'E' 0-4-4Ts of 1896-1901, three of which were built at Neasden. A new styling was applied where all the information was given on elliptical brass numberplates on the bunker. These numberplates had two raised rims forming a border, within which was "METROPOLITAN RAILWAY" over and "BUILT [date] NEASDEN WORKS" under the central seriffed number. The tanksides were left unlettered, and reverted to three panels of lining, despite the tanks being one smooth sheet, each rectangle having decorative incurved corners to the lining. The Met's first armorial device featuring two tunnel mouths was applied to the front sandboxes.

The Class 'F' 0-6-2Ts of 1901 reverted to the painted tankside number, but retained the three panels of decorated lining, which also appeared on several other engines repainted during this period.

Mr Clark's successor Mr Charles Jones at first made few changes, except that the decorative corners to the lining were abandoned. From circa 1903 all front bufferbeams carried "M [hook] R" in seriffed gold letters shaded in black, and brass domes were generally painted over. A handsome new armorial device was introduced about 1905, consisting of a shield quartered with the arms of London, Middlesex, Hertford and Buckingham surrounded by a great deal of elaborate crimson mantling edged in ermine. The crest was a hand holding bolts of electricity, and the motto below carried the words "METROPOLITAN RAILWAY".

The Class 'G' 0-6-4Ts of 1916 introduced a new style. Numbers were on rectangular brass numberplates carried on the bunker, with vermilion backgrounds, chimney numbers being abandoned. Tanks were lined in a single panel, with the device in the centre. The company name was disposed as "METROPOLITAN" curved over the top of the device and "RAILWAY" curved under. The lettering was now smaller and sans-serif, and photographs would suggest it was shaded in blue. Bufferbeams were not lettered. Names appeared on small curved brass plates on the front splashers.

365
Metropolitan Railway

Locomotive front bufferbeams 1903-1916.

366
Metropolitan Railway

Simplified lettering circa 1903-circa 1925.

New locomotive lettering 1916-1921 for Class 'G' 0-6-4T and Class 'H' 4-4-4T.

Neasdon shed in 1907: 0-4-4T No. 82 is at the front, then 4-4-0T No. 41, with an anonymous 0-6-0 saddle tank at the rear.
Author's collection

Metropolitan Railway

Metropolitan Railway 0-6-4T No. 94 Lord Aberconway was built in 1915 by the Yorkshire Engine Co. Ltd of Sheffield for passenger services on the Aylsbury Extension Line. *Author's collection*

The Class 'H' 4-4-4Ts of 1920 followed this style, although they were not named. The 4-4-0Ts repainted during this period were also affected; tanks were lined in a single panel and were lettered "METROPOLITAN [device] RAILWAY" in the smaller sans-serif characters, shaded in blue, shadowed in black.

From 1921 a new style began to appear which became the postwar standard. Tanks were now universally lined in a single panel. The name was shortened to "METROPOLITAN" painted in a straight line, with a large painted number below and the device on the bunker. Large painted numbers also appeared on the rear of bunkers. All numbers now had the class designation below in small capitals (A to K). The Class 'K' 2-6-4Ts of 1925 had no number on the tanks (having brass numberplates) and this became the final style: "METROPOLITAN" alone on the tanksides, and all numbers (painted or brass plate) on the bunker. All lettering was straw, now shaded to right and below in black, except on the rear numbers, which seem to be shaded in black to the left. The device was no longer used.

The Met became part of the LPTB in 1933, but little seems to have been done until 1934. Two engines (No. 91 and No. 105) are known to have received "MET." on their tanks, and numbers began to appear on front buffer beams. From about the middle of 1934 "LONDON TRANSPORT" appeared gradually on engines, but Classes 'G', 'H' and 'K' were sold to the L&NER in 1937 and thereafter appeared in that company's standard black livery. The London Transport locomotive colour is alleged to have been that of the Met, but in my opinion it later became considerably browner.

The Metropolitan's first carriages were finished in varnished teak. The styling was unusual and copied from the contemporary

Metropolitan Railway 0-6-2T No. 93. *Author's collection*

Metropolitan Railway

broad gauge GWR carriages, being 38ft 6ins long and rigid, despite having two outer radial axles, their length earning them the nick-name of 'long charleys'. First class carriages were cream (white under varnish) above the waist, but only for the extent of the First class accommodation, apparently lined with fine red and blue lines. Generally, lining was 'gold' or a yellow equivalent. Standard gauge rigid carriages were purchased from Brown, Marshall in 1863, and were fitted with the well-known 'round top' doors from 1868. By 1884 the rigid carriages were causing trouble on the District's sharp curves and their replacement was recommended. Fortunately the Met were considering new stock for the extension to Rickmansworth. The carriages ordered had a length of 27ft 6ins but a wheelbase of only 14ft 0ins. They were marshalled in block trains of eight or nine carriages: typically Bk.2nd/2nd/1st/1st/3rd/3rd/3rd/3rd/Bk.3rd. Due to the date of their appearance,1887, they were of course known as the 'Jubilee' stock. They were the first Met carriages to have a 'turn under' at the waist.

Electrification changed the face of the Met for ever. All previous stock was superseded by six 9-coach sets of what was known as 'bogie stock'. Twenty 'Bo-Bo' electric locomotives were purchased in 1906 of what was often called the 'camel back' type. In the same year, two four-carriage sets were converted into self-powered electric units, known as the 'N Stock'.

Lining was in yellow, fine-lined on each side with vermilion. The twenty 'Bo-Bo' electric locomotives were painted dark red [1] and lined in yellow. They were decorated with the company device at each end, with the number centrally, e.g "No 1".

Carriage lettering was symmetrical, the name originally being on two lines, "METROPOLITAN" above "RAILWAY" and flanked by two numbers, all sans–serif in gold shaded black. Class marking was in numerals "1ST" and so on. This remained the lettering style until the appearance of the electric '1905 stock'. These carriages were varnished teak, with cream (white under varnish) on waist panels, upright panels and eaves panels. The steam stock remained varnished teak, now no longer with white above the waist for First class. Lettering was still symmetrical; "(number) METROPOLITAN RAILWAY (number)" in gold serif characters, blocked in blue to the left and shaded black, with the device below each number. Lining was in 'gold', but by this stage this was probably a straw-coloured equivalent. Class marking was in serif numerals in the waist, the suffixed abbreviations being abandoned. Wheel tyres were painted white.

From 1910 all stock was now teak, steel panels on electric stock being painted and grained to match. Lettering styles remained the same. In the 1930s, it seems that the company name was shortened to "METROPOLITAN" centrally to match the steam locomotives, and lining was restricted to waist and eaves panels. The new

369
Metropolitan Railway

Metropolitan Railway 'E' Class 0-4-4T condensing engine No. 77 with a 6-coach set of 'Ashbury' bogie carriages at Neasden in 1905.
Author's collection

Metropolitan Railway

First Class carriage No. 43 at Chesham, with white upper panels and the name painted on two lines.   Author's collection

Metropolitan Vickers electric locomotives were painted and lined just as before.

Non-passenger carriage stock, of which there was a small number, was varnished wood or painted and grained to match, with limited lining. A horsebox photographed in the 1930s was lettered "METROPOLITAN" across the drop part of the door in yellow or 'straw', with the large number "10" below. In small script on the bottom plank was "*To carry 3 Tons*" and its home station "*Wendover*". It is likely that earlier lettering included the word "RAILWAY", as was standard on the carriages.

Goods stock was painted a medium grey. In the earlier period there was no body lettering. The numberplate was semicircular and fitted inside the solebar crownplates, the company name in full arching over the number. By circa 1900, wagon sides bore the abbreviation "MET." in large letters (approximately 14 inches), although it seems the outside-frame cattle wagons were lettered "MET. [door] RLY." in a smaller size to fit the available space. Full stops used on the abbreviations were square and quite prominent. Numbers were painted on the lower right of the body, and tare was usually on the left.

A British Thompson Houston locomotive and train from Baker Street to Aylesbury, racing a Great Central Railway train from Marylebone.   Author's collection

371
Metropolitan Railway

The later Metropolitan-Vickers type of locomotive, introduced in 1923-24, on a train to Rickmansworth. *Author's collection*

One of the first electric multiple units is seen in this postcard which was posted August 1906. *Author's collection*

372
Metropolitan Railway

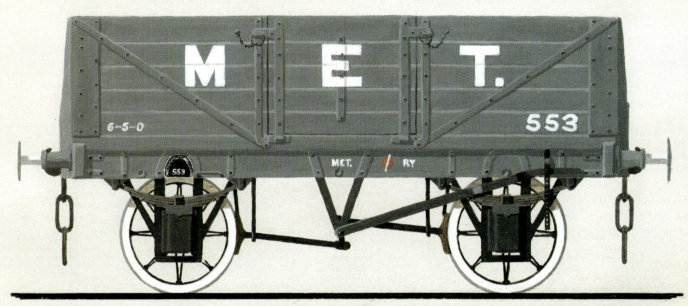

Metropolitan 0-4-4T No. 41 stands at Quainton Road with a mixed train to Brill in August 1935.
Author's collection

Brake vans carried "MET." with the number centrally below, on both sides and ends, the latter being painted vermilion. Many wagons carried a red circle crossed by an oblique white line on the solebar, as a prohibition against use in the tunnels between Finchley Road and Baker Street. Some wagons seem not to have had numberplates, "MET.RY." and the number being painted on the solebar. Wheel tyres were painted white.

Wagon sheets are noted in 1896 as having "METROPOLITAN RAILWAY" down the centre of the sheet, with "MET.RLY." and the number in each corner, which themselves were painted red.

| 1 | 'MIDLAND CRIMSON' CARTER 28 PANTONE 188C BS 381 C 540 'CRIMSON' |

North London Railway

The East & West India Docks and Birmingham Junction Railway was incorporated in 1846 for a line from the London & North Western Railway at Camden (Chalk Farm) to the London & Blackwall Railway and the Docks. The new company was to have its own dock at Poplar. Construction was slow, and the line was opened in sections, the last in January 1852. Thankfully, the name was changed a year later to the North London Railway. The NLR had been envisaged as chiefly a goods line, which function it fulfilled admirably, giving easy access to the docks for the L&NWR, Great Northern Railway and Midland Railway, but its passenger traffic grew rapidly. Accordingly, a City terminus at Broad Street was opened in 1865, half of it used by the L&NWR. The L&NWR always had a major interest in the NLR; sixteen of its twenty-four directors were L&NWR appointees, and it subscribed two thirds of the capital.

The growth in suburban traffic was largely thanks to the North & South Western Junction Railway, opened in 1853, and the Hampstead Junction Railway, opened in 1860. Neither of these lines was owned by the NLR, although it was a joint partner in the N&SWJ with the L&NWR and MR, but it took a large part in the passenger working. The GNR was struggling with its own suburban traffic and, as the L&NWR would not allow the GNR access to Broad Street, the NLR began a service over the GNR lines in 1875. The result of all its running powers meant that, although it owned only 12 miles of track, and part-owned five more, the NLR services covered over 40 miles around London. At their furthest extent, NLR trains reached Richmond (15 miles from Broad Street), on what was termed the 'Outer Circle', to distinguish it from the 'Inner Circle' of the Metropolitan and the District railways.

The 19th century was a secure time for the NLR, but in the new century, competition from electric trams and the deep tube railways caused a decline in traffic. From February 1909 the L&NWR took over the management of the railway and the resultant economies partly arrested the decline. Electric traction was introduced in 1916, and the railway was finally absorbed by the L&NWR in 1922.

For the first decade, locomotives were supplied by outside builders or the L&NWR, but from 1863 Bow Works, under the superintendence of Mr William Adams, built its own engines. Mr Adams moved to the Great Eastern Railway in 1873, to be replaced by Mr John C. Park. From 1893 Mr Henry J. Pryce filled the post, until the L&NWR took over in 1909.

The North London Railway became a part of the London Midland & Scottish Railway in 1923, and passed into the London Midland Region of British Railways in 1948.

Originally, locomotives were a light green [1], lined out in black and white. Tanks and other panels were edged in black with curved corners rather than right-angles, fine-lined in white. The main lining usually had incurved corners. The frames and valances have been described as 'deep vermilion', which is of course nonsense. They were almost certainly a red-brown such as Indian red, lined out in black and vermilion. Domes were polished brass and chimneys had polished copper caps. There were large numberplates on the

No. 88, from the Railway Magazine (August 1902). — Author's collection

374
North London Railway

NLR 4-4-0T No. 113. Author's collection

375
North London Railway

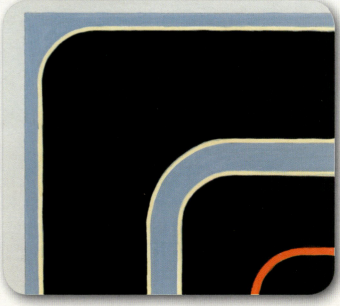

Locomotive lining panel.

tanksides, carrying "NORTH LONDON" over and "RAILWAY" under the central number, in brass with a vermilion background. The number was also placed on the chimney front in cut-out brass numerals.

There were several changes in the early part of Mr Park's tenure. A new design of rectangular numberplate was introduced, the lining used normal corners, and a number of engines on the duplicate list (numbered upwards from 101) were painted black, lined in vermilion. However, it was from 1885 that the most far-reaching change occurred, when all locomotives were painted black, with a new lining scheme.

Body panels and valances were edged with blue-grey, fine-lined with light yellow on the inner edges (possibly white under varnish). On the tanks and bunkers were panels of blue-grey, edged on both sides with yellow. At a distance inside the lining was a fine line of vermilion. Boiler bands were lined in vermilion only, as were the outside bogie frames of the inside-cylinder '43' Class and '51' Class 4-4-0 tanks. Outside cylinders were incorporated with the smokebox wrapper plate and were not lined. Buffer beams were vermilion, edged in black, possibly with the drawhook plate painted black as well. Numbers were applied in the usual form

376
North London Railway

NLR 4-4-0T No. 120 is seen with decorated chimney at Acton, 18th May 1901.   Author's collection

"Nº [hook] 88" for example, in gold seriffed characters shaded in black. Buffer casings were vermilion, with a black outer lip. The ends of the wooden bufferbeams were painted black, but outlined with the blue-grey and yellow, and lined vermilion. The brass numberplates were outlined with more blue-grey and yellow. Below this on the outside-cylinder 4-4-0 tanks was placed the armorial device. The device incorporated the arms of the East India Dock, Birmingham, City of London and West India Dock inside a blue garter carrying the name of the company.

The motion and inner faces of the frames were painted vermilion, as were coupling rods. Wheels were lined in vermilion on the inner edge of the tyres, around the boss and the axle ends. Each spoke also had a vermilion line up its centre.

After the L&NWR take-over, locomotive lining assumed the typical L&NWR form; a blue-grey line edged on the inside with white, and a vermilion line a short distance inside. The panel edging was abandoned. Some NLR engines made over to L&NWR stock actually received standard L&NWR brass numberplates. Locos remaining in NLR stock had the bufferbeam numerals painted out and the Crewe rectangle of black lining placed there instead, although they retained the Bow black edge to the buffer casings. Ends of bufferbeams were plain black.

NLR 0-6-0T No. 80 in original green livery.   Author's collection

377
North London Railway

NLR 4-4-0T No. 50 outside the shed at Bow.　　　　　　　　　　　　　　　　　　　　　　　　　　　Author's collection

NLR 4-4-0T No. 71 at Bow, 11th August 1923.　　　　　　　　　　　　　　　　　　　　　　　　　　Author's collection

North London Railway

Carriages were all 4-wheeled, and were always built of teak and varnished, with no lining. Solebars were also varnished wood, and ironwork thereon was 'bronze brown' instead of black. Vehicles later fitted with solebar flitch plates had these painted 'teak' brown to match. Roofs were white when new, with gas-lamp tops painted black. Rather than have gas tanks under each vehicle, gas was kept in cylinders in each brake van, with the pipes and connections along the roofs. Wheels were the wood-centred Mansell pattern, varnished at first but probably painted 'teak' brown later, and iron parts were black. The carriages were arranged into close-coupled sets with brake vans at each end. These had raised lookouts, and their outer ends were painted vermilion.

Lettering was in gold sans-serif characters outlined in two methods. First class vehicles had lettering edged in white, followed by a black line, then an outer blue line. Other classes had white, black and a red outer line instead. All classes had the class marking in words on each door "FIRST", "SECOND" or "THIRD", but class changed the approach to other details. Most vehicles had elliptical wooden roundels on the doors, and on First class carriages the armorial device was placed there. Second class had a gold script rendering of "NLR". Third class, at least by the 1890s, had a large seriffed "3" with a flat top. Numbers were placed on the eaves panels. On five-compartment vehicles where there was a central door, it was applied in the form "N^o [door] 114" for example. Four-compartment carriages simply had a central numeral without a prefix.

Luggage Brakes had lettering on the lower body "LUGGAGE VAN [number]", and some also had "N L R" in the panels above the waist. The guard's doors carried "GUARD'S COMP^T".

When the L&NWR built some new sets of 4-wheeled carriages in 1910-12, they also used varnished teak, but solebars were black, and brake ends were not vermilion. The beading was different, too, and a new lettering style was used in the waist panels; still outlined in the former way, but now seriffed. The arrangement was to have two numbers placed symmetrically, with devices below. On each door, large seriffed class numerals were placed, similar to those the L&NWR used on its 'Outer Circle' sets, the "3" having a rounded top.

There are references to NLR wagons being a dark grey 'almost black', but this is patently untrue. Goods wagons were a medium

North London Railway

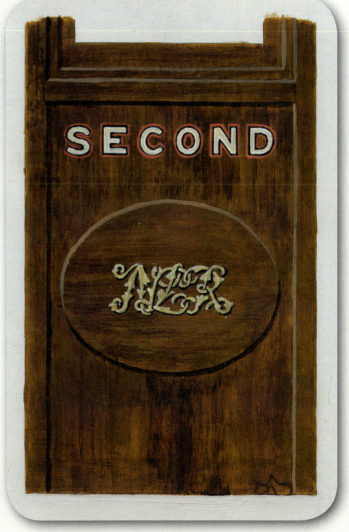

Treatment of Second class NLR carriage.

grey, similar to the L&NWR wagon grey, with black below the solebar. Newly-built wagons photographed outside Bow Works have body strapping and buffer casings painted japan black, and traces on the few photographs that show wagons in traffic would suggest that this finish was the standard one. The size of the wagon stock was not large; in 1907 there were 516 units, almost entirely mineral wagons and brakes.

The standard solebar numberplate was rectangular with rounded corners, having "N.L.R." with full stops over the central number, and "BOW ROAD WORKS" and the date underneath. This was normally positioned to the right of centre. Another, smaller plate over the left-hand wheel denoted the maximum load.

Lettering on open wagons was "N.L.R" with square full stops, positioned on the upper left portion of the side, with the number on the corresponding position to the right. The letters took up all of one plank height, approximately 9 inches. Loco coal wagons had additional lettering below, with "LOCO' DEP^T" on the left in about 4½-inch characters, and "BOW" to the right in 6-inch letters. Tare was painted on the bottom left of the lowest plank. Brake vans, which had white roofs, had their lettering placed centrally on the

380 North London Railway

side, with "N.L.R" over the number. The company possessed no wagon sheets.

After the L&NWR took over the operation of the railway, wagons retained their NLR livery but had a rectangular plate fixed on the body lettered "LNWR", and it became usual to paint the maximum load on the body in the L&NWR manner.

1 'Adams Green'
Carter 7
Pantone 364C
RAL 6010
'Grass Green'

NLR 0-6-0T in photographic livery at Bow with brake No. 1003 and open No. 127 in the background. Author's collection

Somerset & Dorset Joint Railway

The Somerset & Dorset Railway was the result of an amalgamation in 1862 of the Somerset Central Railway (incorporated 1852 as a broad gauge line) and the Dorset Central Railway (incorporated 1855 as a standard gauge line). The SCR opened from Highbury to Glastonbury in 1854, worked by the broad gauge Bristol & Exeter Railway. Extensions to Burnham and to Wells were opened in 1858 and 1859 respectively. The DCR opened in 1860 and ran from Wimborne on the London & South Western Railway northwards to Blandford, worked by the L&SWR.

The two railways realised that it would be advantageous to join forces and a line to link the two systems was authorised in 1857. The SCR would extend (using mixed gauge) from Glastonbury to Cole, near Bruton, where the DCR would also extend to meet them, crossing the L&SWR at Templecombe. The Somerset Central commenced working of the railway between Burnham and Templecombe in February of 1862, and in September of that year the Somerset & Dorset Railway was incorporated. The final part of the through line was completed from Blandford to Templecombe in August 1863. The broad gauge third rail of the mixed gauge had been removed by about 1870.

The financial situation quickly became serious; the S&DR was in receivership between 1866 and 1870. The Directors thought that the only way to save the company was to build a difficult line over the Mendip Hills from Evercreech Junction to the Midland Railway at Bath. An Act was obtained in 1871, and the line opened in July 1874, but the S&DR's finances were exhausted and selling was the only option.

After an unpromising offer from the Bristol & Exeter Railway, the S&DR accepted a joint offer from the Midland and London & South Western railways, who agreed to lease the line as the Somerset & Dorset Joint Railway from 1st November 1875. This arrangement was confirmed by an Act of July 1876.

The joint line was steadily improved. Through working was extended to the new Bournemouth station in June 1874, and a south-facing loop line was opened in 1885 between Corfe Mullen Junction and Broadstone Junction on the L&SWR to avoid reversal of through trains at Wimborne. Several sections were doubled, but a great deal remained single line. Finally, a branch to Bridgwater opened in 1890. The length of line in 1901 was 100 miles 60 chains, of which 38 miles was double track.

The S&DJR had its own works at Highbridge. Although under the control of the Midland Railway officers at Derby (in turn Samuel Waite Johnson, Richard Deeley and Henry Fowler), Highbridge had a degree of freedom and Resident Locomotive Superintendents of its own: B.S. Fisher (1876-83), W.H. French (1883-89), Alfred Whitaker (1889-1911), F. Ryan (1911-13) and R.C. Archbutt (1913-30). The most famous was of course Alfred Whitaker, who invented an automatic tablet exchanger for single line working.

The joint arrangements continued after the Grouping, although now between the London Midland & Scottish Railway and the Southern Railway, until the separate management of the line was discontinued in 1930 and Highbridge Works closed. At Nationalisation, the S&DJR was allocated to the Southern Region of British Railways, hence its presence in this volume. From 1958

Somerset & Dorset Joint Railway Class '69' 4-4-0 No. 77, built at Derby in March 1908. Author's collection

382
Somerset & Dorset Joint Railway

the section north of Templecombe was passed to the Western Region.

The original colour of S&DR locomotives was dark green, relieved by polished brass and copper. Most were 2-4-0s built by George England & Co, the company name and number appearing on each splasher in brass characters, for example "S&DR" and "Nº10", each arranged in a curve. The lettering "S & [hook] D R" appeared on the front bufferbeam. The only exception to the green livery was the 2-4-0T No. 11, which was delivered in the standard George England blue colour and nicknamed *Bluebottle*. This engine had painted lettering and numbers "S&DR Nº11" in a straight line on the tanks.

After the Midland Railway assumed responsibility for locomotives in 1876, all new engines were to Derby designs, unmistakably Johnson engines but usually modified with smaller wheels for use on the steep gradients of the S&DJR.

Painting followed the current standard Midland livery. This was initially the lighter green lined in black and white introduced by Mr Johnson at Derby, followed in turn by the crimson lined in black and yellow introduced in 1883. Lining details and 6½-inch brass numerals were typically Midland, and there were no company initials.

It is believed that March 1886 was the adoption date of the dark blue livery [1]. In my opinion, the colour patch (number 26) in E.F. Carter's *Britain's Railway Liveries* is abysmal, not resembling any recorded mixture or formula described below in this chapter. The S&DJR blue is often called 'Prussian blue' in modern references, but contemporary sources only refer to blue or dark blue, and C. Hamilton Ellis refers to 'Royal blue' (*The Trains We Loved*).

A specification of 1890 reveals a layered method. After three coats of lead colour (grey), there was one of dark blue (Prussian blue with a little white lead), then two coats of ultramarine and four coats of varnish. This is similar to the practice on the Caledonian Railway, where a 'blue ground' based on Prussian blue was used below the ultramarine, which is a very transparent pigment in oil. The Great Eastern Railway had to use four coats of ultramarine on a light grey undercoat to achieve their blue. Tellingly, the railway artist E.W. Twining recommended the use of Carter's colour patch No. 24, which is the same as that provided for the GER blue.

The painting and lining of the locomotives generally followed the Midland manner. Dark blue was applied to all the engine, including boiler, cab front and sides, splashers, wheels, frames, guard irons, sandboxes, tenders and tender frames. Smokebox, chimney, splasher tops, platform (footplate) and cab roof were black. Tender fronts

383 Somerset & Dorset Joint Railway

and tops were also black, as were brake gear and springs, but spring buckles and tender axlebox fronts were dark blue and lined.

Boiler bands were black, and body panels, tanksides, bunkers and splashers were edged in black. Below the platform, valances, steps, main frames, tender frames, guard irons and sandboxes were also edged in black. All of this was fine-lined with a ¼ inch lemon chrome (yellow) line between the black and the dark blue. Wheels had the wheel-centres edged in black, black tyres and axle ends, all fine-lined in lemon chrome.

In addition to the lined black edging, tanks, cab side sheets (lower and upper where present) and tenders were lined with panels of black fine-lined on each side in yellow, to make bands two inches wide. Tanks were lined with one panel, but the Johnson tenders had two panels on the side, and one on the rear.

There was at first no company lettering, except on bufferbeams. The bufferbeams or buffer plates themselves were painted vermilion [2], lined in black and fine-lined yellow. Upon them were applied the large letters "S D [hook] J R" in gold sans-serif characters shaded in blue and white, shadowed in black, which also appeared on the rear bufferbeams of tank engines.

By 1891 the company initials were appearing on tenders in typical Midland style, being 6½-inch gold seriffed characters, shaded in dark blue, light blue and white, shadowed in black. Midland-type tenders had a vertical beading strip that was not quite central, the rear panel being slightly longer than the forward one. The initials "S D | J R" were disposed in such a manner that the letters were the same distance from the nearest lining and therefore not equidistant. Overall width (between centres) was about 14 feet.

From this time the armorial device was also applied to driving wheel splashers of passenger locomotives, or centrally on tanksides. Lettering on tanks was spaced accordingly, "S D [device] J R", to incorporate it.

The armorial device itself was 9 inches wide by 12 inches high, formed from the arms of Bath (on the left) and Dorchester (on the right) enclosed in a light blue garter, on which was the wording "SOMERSET & DORSET JOINT RAILWAY" in gilt letters.

Midland seriffed 6½-inch numerals were universally applied. Engines on the duplicate list had a small 'A' placed next to the number. The usual position on tender engines was on the lower cab side or on the rear splashers. Tank engines had the number on the bunker, except some of the earlier examples which had their numbers in the Midland position centrally on the tanks. In these cases the lettering was spaced accordingly, for example "S D 13 J R", and the device was placed above.

Somerset & Dorset Joint Railway

Class 'C' 0-4-4T No. 55, built at the Vulcan Foundry in January 1885 and seen at Bath before 1906. *Author's collection*

Derby continually sought to improve the motive power of the S&DJR, delivering the beautiful Class 'A' 4-4-0s in 1891-97 and the Class '69' 4-4-0s with large round-topped 'H' boilers in 1903. On the freight side, five of the standard Midland '2284' Class were built by Derby in 1896 and nick-named 'Bulldogs'. A second batch of five were delivered in 1902 carrying Midland crimson lake livery but lettered "S D J R", being part of an order diverted by Derby to the joint line.

When Mr Deeley succeeded Mr Johnson and introduced simplified styles at Derby in 1905, the practice at Highbridge changed similarly. The panels of lining on tenders and cabs disappeared, leaving only the black and yellow edging, although boiler bands were all still painted black and lined in yellow. Johnson tenders now had the wide beading on the tankside painted black and lined on its inner edge with yellow, but ignoring the central vertical. The lettering "S D J R", although still about 14 feet in extent, now also ignored the central beading and was equidistantly spaced. Below the platform, valances, steps and tender frames were still blue, edged in black and yellow, but wheels, frames, guard irons and sandboxes were now black with no lining, except a single line of yellow around the inner edge of the wheel tyres.

Mr (later Sir Henry) Fowler took charge at Derby in 1910, where he introduced black for goods locomotives. Thus when the first Derby-built Class '80' 2-8-0s arrived in 1914 they were painted unlined black, with unlettered bufferbeams and smokebox door numberplates. They were delivered with transfer numerals on the cabside, and the initials "SDJR" closely-spaced on the sides of the tender. Highbridge rectified the inconsistencies with brass numerals and initials spaced out in the usual manner.

Goods engines from this date began to be turned out from Highbridge in unlined black, although no other smokebox door numbers appeared as yet. Derby also supplied more new engines; the five standard MR Class '3835' 0-6-0s (later '4F') supplied by Armstrong, Whitworth in 1921 were delivered painted black, but with closely-spaced tender initials and transfer numerals. Once again Highbridge rectified the deficiency.

The black livery was not necessarily consistently applied. All of the 'Bulldog' 0-6-0s were rebuilt with 'G7' boilers from 1920 but, strangely, the first three to be rebuilt were turned out of Highbridge in lined dark blue.

Most of the Class '69' 4-4-0s and two of the Class 'A' 4-4-0s were 'rebuilt' at Derby between 1914 and 1921 into the superheated Midland Class '483'. This so-called rebuilding has been questioned, as there cannot have been any of the original engines left. All the S&DJR Class '483' engines arrived from Derby in the simplified blue livery, with smokebox door numbers and transfer numerals. These were replaced at Highbridge by brass numerals.

There were also several detail changes in this period. Firstly, the bufferbeam initials "SD [hook] JR" were now seriffed. Secondly, Highbridge started to attach 2-inch power class lettering on the upper cab sheets in the Midland manner, except that the letters "P" for passenger and "G" for goods were used, as they never were at Derby. The goods power rating was placed below the passenger rating rather than beside it. For example, the Class 'C' 0-4-4Ts

Somerset & Dorset Joint Railway

Class 'A' 4-4-0 No. 45, built at Derby in January 1897 and seen at its home shed of Bath circa 1920.   Author's collection

and the Class 'G' 0-6-0s were "$\frac{1P}{1G}$". Thirdly, it became the practice to paint the home shed in very small capitals, probably in yellow, about halfway up the cab sides, above the handrail or above the step in the panelling, where present.

Another change after the First World War was the method of achieving the blue livery. Rather than the tedious and time-consuming layering of transparent colours, a pre-prepared mixture was applied in one or two coats to the lead colour undercoat before varnishing. Passed on to Raymond Lee by the fomer paint foreman at Highbridge, this formula consisted simply of 9lb ultramarine, ½lb crimson lake, ¼lb purple lake. I believe the latter may actually be 'purple brown', as according to my *Paint and Colour Mixing* by A.S. Jennings, Purple Lake is a light-sensitive watercolour. Using this substitution, the mixture makes an approximation of the original colour. The S&DJR blue is said to have changed latterly, and this mixing method would have been the cause of such a change, lacking the depth of the layered method.

Generally speaking, the Grouping hardly affected the S&DJR. The locomotive liveries remained the same as before 1923, with the detail differences already mentioned. A second batch of Class '80' 2-8-0s built by R. Stephenson & Co. with larger boilers were delivered in plain black in 1925. Derby supplied three of the standard LM&SR Class '563' 4-4-0s (2P) in 1928, in lined blue but without the boiler band painting, and seven 'Jinty' 0-6-0Ts of 1929 built by W.G. Bagnall Ltd in unlined blue. Numbers were applied in transfer numerals and the bufferbeam lettering was finally abandoned.

Several of the newer engines with higher numbers were renumbered downwards into vacant spaces in 1928. The new numbers were applied in transfers, the old brass numerals being taken away. Some goods engines had transfer numerals on a plate fixed to the engine. This was probably to conceal the scars where the former brass figures had been removed, without wasting time rubbing them down in the paintshop.

The decision was finally taken in 1929 to paint all locomotives black, but the only passenger locomotive to be treated in this way seems to have been Class 'A' 4-4-0 No. 18 (formerly No. 45) in May 1929. The Highbridge Works officially closed on 31st December 1929 and the LM&SR took over the locomotive stock from 1st January 1930.

The LM&SR renumbered the surviving engines. Because Highbridge was permitted to complete all work in hand until March 1930, several locomotives received their new LM&SR number and lettering "L M S" while still in their blue livery. Ultimately, all ex-S&DJR engines were painted black.

The original carriages of the Somerset & Dorset Railway were 4-wheeled, and a handful of these survived into the 20th century. From the 1880s, the Midland arranged orders of their standard 6-wheeled types from contractors. These carriages were of typical Midland outline, with deep eaves panels and shallow waist panels, arc roofs and turn-unders at the sides and ends. From 1885, similar carriages were built at Highbridge, although they evolved some designs that Derby never actually produced.

386
Somerset & Dorset Joint Railway

It is believed that carriages were originally a 'chocolate' shade similar to that of the Midland (i.e. dark red or crimson). After 1876 carriages were certainly dark red, and their lining was very probably the same as that on the Midland.

From 1886 carriages were painted the same dark blue [1] as the locomotives. The painting specification was identical to that of the Midland, merely with blue replacing crimson. All fascia (beading) was painted black with a ⅜-inch gold line around the edges and a

Bogie Brake Third No. 100, built Highbridge in 1904 and scrapped in February 1935.   Author's collection

Somerset & Dorset Joint Railway

fine ⅛-inch vermilion line between the gold and the black. Carriage ends were dark blue with the fascia painted black. Roofs and roof fittings were lead colour.

Solebars were dark blue with a wide black edge, lined gold, and with an inner line of vermilion. Below the solebar was black, with varnished teak-centred wheels. Footboards were also black. Some of the old 4-wheeled carriages had applied beading rather than mouldings, and these featured a central gold line on the beading.

Lettering was on the waist in standard Midland-type characters, being 2-inch gold sans-serif letters and numbers, shaded in red and white, shadowed in black. Class marking was in words "FIRST", "THIRD" and occasionally "SECOND" throughout the S&DJR period. Other wording included "GUARD" and "PASSENGERS LUGGAGE" on the appropriate doors.

Positioning of company initials, numbers and armorial devices depended on length and type of carriage. Six-wheeled stock with four compartments (Firsts and a few Composites) had the number central with the device below, and "S&DJR" on the panels on each side. Six-wheeled Thirds had five compartments; the majority of the Composites followed the Midland design with two compartments on each side of a central luggage compartment. On both these types of vehicles the number occurred twice, once on each side of the central compartment, with "S&DJR" also twice on the flanking panels at each side. Thirds had a device on the central door, but Composites had a device on the two First class doors.

Highbridge started building bogie carriages in 1898, the first one or two being straight copies of Midland carriages with arc roofs, but then Highbridge adopted the L&SWR semi-elliptical roof for all subsequent construction, bogie and six-wheel, which carried on until 1913. Painting was as above, even to the detail on solebars, but bogies were black. From about 1912, gold lining on all carriages was replaced by yellow ochre, and it is probable that solebars were painted black from this date too, as on the Midland.

Lettering on the bogie vehicles followed a more standard arrangement. There were two numbers either side of a central compartment, with the company initials "S&DJR" on the panels beyond on each side, below which were the two devices.

Passenger-rated vehicles, including milk vans, carriage trucks and horseboxes, were all painted dark blue and lined in black and yellow. Lettering was also in yellow, shaded in red and shadowed in black. Horseboxes and carriage trucks had the initials and number placed close together, for example "S&DJR Nº11". The milk vans, which were of more passenger carriage outline, but with square-cornered fascia, had three double doors with louvres per side, and the initials

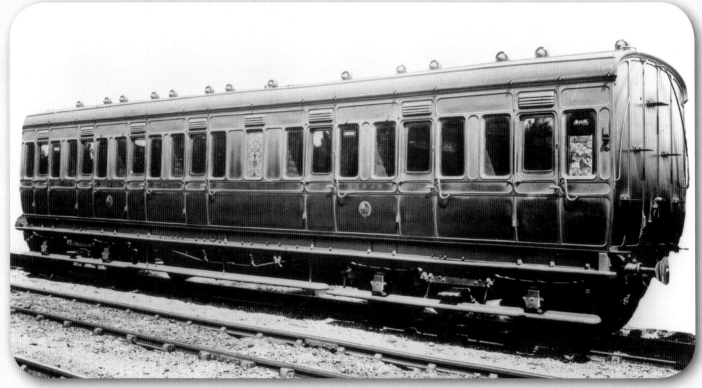
Seven-compartment Bogie Lavatory Third No. 90, built at Highbridge in 1900 and scrapped in 1939. *Author's collection*

Four-wheeled 10-ton goods brake No. 34, built Highbridge October 1886 and scrapped in 1913. The tare of 10t 2 0 is carved into the left-hand end of the bottom rail and the plate is of the earlier Midland type, the later plates were bigger. *Author's collection*

Somerset & Dorset Joint Railway

and number were placed on each side of the central door. The device was placed below the number.

Just as for the locomotives, the Grouping had little effect, except that it is believed that carriage ends were now plain blue, just as LM&SR carriages had plain crimson ends. In 1930 the carriage stock was split between the LM&SR and the Southern Railway, but did not survive long in its new guise, partly due to all the ex-S&DJR stock being gas-lit.

Although Derby did supply some of their design of wagons, Highbridge built most of their own goods stock. Wagons were painted light grey, with ironwork on the body painted black japan, but only selected pieces of ironwork on the solebar were black, such as the brake 'vee' hangers, and sometimes crown plates. Below the solebar was black.

Lettering was white, about 6 inches high, and normally featured "S&DJR" on the left of the body, with the number on the right, preceded by "Nº". Open wagons were normally lettered on the second plank up from the bottom rail. Covered vans were lettered on the second plank down from the top. Tare was originally painted on the bottom rail or on the solebar in italic script lettering, for example "*Tare 5.4.2*".

Goods brake vans were at first 10-ton 4-wheeled vans, but subsequently Highbridge built 20-ton 6-wheeled vans to cope with the gradients of the Bath extension. Brake vans were lettered on the second plank down from the top, with tare on the bottom rail. Some of the older vans actually had the company initials and number carved into the bottom rail.

It should be mentioned that some official photographs show black shading to the lettering, but this was for photographic purposes only, as were white tyres.

At first there were no numberplates, except a very small elliptical builder's plate centrally on the solebar. However, from about 1895 a cast iron numberplate was applied to the solebar, or sometimes on the bottom rail. This had incurved corners like the Midland plates,

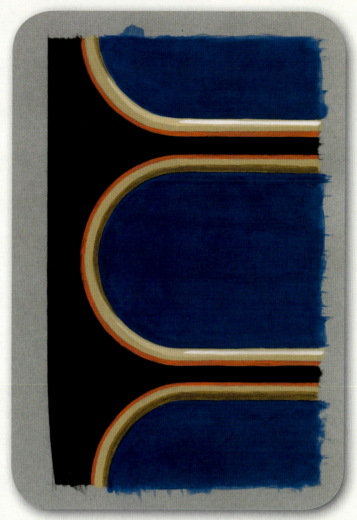

S&DJR carriage lining.

Six-wheeled 20-ton brake van No. 6 was built in 1890 and was probably photographed when new. Author's collection

390 Somerset & Dorset Joint Railway

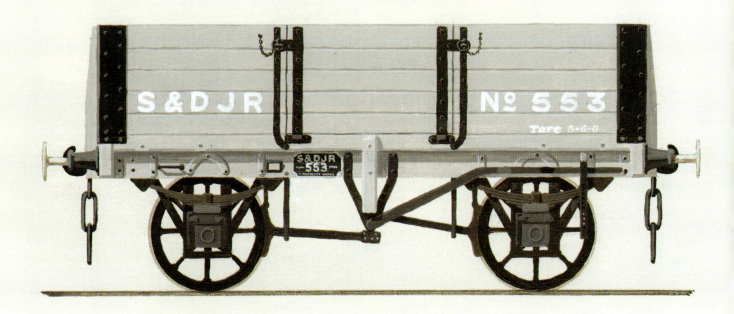

and was in two forms. The first was the same size as a Midland plate, with "S&DJR" over the vehicle number, but the second form was larger, applied only to wagons built at Highbridge. Between the initials and the number was "BUILDERS", with "HIGHBRIDGE WORKS" below the number. On each side of the number was the month and year of construction. When plates were supplied, tare lettering moved up onto the lower right body of open wagons.

In 1914, it was agreed that the revenue-earning goods stock was to be distributed equally between the Midland Railway and the L&SWR, leaving only peat wagons, locomotive coal wagons, brake vans and service stock still under S&DJR control.

Until 1914, it is believed service stock was painted red oxide, with black ironwork, as seen on Engineer's Ballast Brake Van No. 1. After 1914, it is thought the remaining service vehicles were now painted dark grey. Service stock featured the wording "ENGINEER'S DEPARTMENT" centrally, and had "*To be returned to Glastonbury*" in script lettering on the solebar.

Wagon sheets are reported as being lettered "S & D J R", with the sheet number, but no other distinguishing marks. A view behind Class 'A' 4-4-0 No. 18 at Bournemouth West shows a more complex design than that implied by that simple Railway Clearing House summary. The usual black-painted canvas approximately 20 x 15 feet in size was used. On it, the initials were painted in about 24-inch seriffed letters on each long side "S & D J", but in place of the expected "R" was a number painted vertically. This lined up exactly with the "S" of the initials on the further side of the sheet. Centrally below the initials (directly below the "D") was the number in about 15-inch seriffed numerals. It is possible there was smaller lettering in the corners, but the details are too indistinct to draw a conclusion.

1	'Dark blue' Carter 24 Pantone 7463C BS 4800 20 C 40 'Midnight'	2	'Vermilion' Carter 36 Pantone 485C BS 4800 04 E 53 'Poppy Red'

South Eastern & Chatham Railway

In 1899 an extraordinary act of co-operation between two erstwhile rivals was consummated. The South Eastern Railway and the London Chatham & Dover Railway had been in cut-throat competition with one another since the 1860s, in part due to the enmity of the two Chairmen, Sir Edward Watkin and James Staats Forbes, who extended their Metropolitan Railway and District Railway feud into Kent. The two railways had nearly amalgamated in 1875, but it was not until after Watkin's resignation due to ill-health in 1894 that overtures of peace could once more be made. It was agreed that there should be a Managing Committee to work the two railways, consisting of ten SER Directors and six from the LC&DR, with a working agreement assigning 41% of receipts to the LC&DR and 59% to the SER. It was a triumph for Forbes. He was offered the Chairmanship of the new Committee, which was commonly known as the South Eastern & Chatham Railway, but he declined, and so Henry Cosmo Orme Bonser (SER) was appointed. Both James Stirling (SER) and William Kirtley (LC&DR) wished to retire, and Mr Harry S. Wainwright was appointed as Locomotive Superintendent.

Wainwright had an uphill struggle to standardise and modernise the railway. He centred engineering work at the SER's Ashford Works and produced excellent locomotives and carriages. Within a few years the SE&CR was one of the best railways in England.

The SE&CR became a constituent of the Southern Railway at the Grouping of 1923, and passed into the Southern Region of British Railways in 1948.

The year 1899 was a period of experiment with liveries. The overall scheme seems to have been to incorporate features of both the former companies. The standard liveries applied from 1900 are detailed below.

The new locomotive livery, applied to all engines, was gorgeous in the extreme, perhaps marking the zenith of steam locomotive embellishment. The main colour was Brunswick green [1], applied in three coats to wheels, boilers, splashers and all panels above the footplate level. Main frames above and below the footplate, valancing and most other details below the footplate were finished in a red-brown colour referred to as 'dark red'. Inside faces of frames, motion and sanding pipes were vermilion [2], as were the buffer beams, although the buffer castings were dark red. Smokeboxes, footplate, cab roof, step treads, wheel tyres and axle ends were black. Domes, safety valve covers, splasher rims, tube plate cleading and spectacle frames were polished brass, and external copper pipes were also polished. Some classes of engine had polished copper chimney caps. The heraldic device, consisting of the 'arms' of the SER and LC&DR side by side within a riband, was applied to driving wheel splashers of the principal passenger classes. The device's riband

No. 504, from the *Railway Magazine* (August 1907).   Author's collection

South Eastern & Chatham Railway

carried the lettering "THE SOUTH EASTERN AND CHATHAM RAILWAY COMPANIES MANAGING COMMITTEE".

It was the lining that made the livery so exotic. All panels above the footplate, and valances, frames, sand boxes and brake hangers below the footplate were edged with black, with a fine line of vermilion between the black and the panel colour. On tanksides, tenders, large cabs, and even cab doors were panels formed of wide bands of light green, having incurved corners. The outer edges of these bands were lined in vermilion, and the inner edges were lined in yellow. Where space was restricted, particularly on splashers and the small cabs of tank engines, the light green band was narrower, and was in contact with the black edging, divided by a vermilion line. Boiler bands were light green edged in yellow, with vermilion lines a short distance outside. There were vermilion lines around the inner edge of the wheel tyres and the axle ends. Wheel bosses had an outer edge of black, also lined with vermilion. Wheel spokes had a central vermilion line, forked at the boss.

393
South Eastern & Chatham Railway

712

Grey locomotive livery from 1916.

SE&CR 0-4-4 No. 534. Built as LC&DR 'A2' Class No. 75 by Robert Stephenson & Co. in 1893, it is seen at some time before reboilering in 1907. *Author's collection*

The first of the SE&CR 'N' Class 2-6-0s, No. 810, was built at Ashford Works in July 1917. *Author's collection*

South Eastern & Chatham Railway

SE&CR 0-4-4T No. 709, built by Sharp, Stewart in December 1900, stands at Longhedge shed on 16th June 1923.
Author's collection

Valancing and step irons, and main frames above the footplate, in addition to the black and red edging had an inner line of yellow. Bufferbeams were edged with black with a fine yellow inner line. Buffer castings were edged at the outer and inner ends with black, lined vermilion and yellow.

The elliptical brass numberplates on constituent engines were replaced by new plates positioned on the bunkers. The central number was surrounded by "SOUTH EASTERN &" above and "CHATHAM RAILWAY" below, with the maker in very small letters under the number. Backgrounds were dark red. Tanks and tenders now carried the letters "S E & C R" in 6-inch gold sans-serif characters, blocked in red, pink and white, shadowed in black. From 1901 new engines carried numbers in 7½-inch cut-out brass numerals on bunkers or cabsides. Buffer beams carried the numbers in the usual "Nº [hook] number", the superscript "O" being underlined and supplemented by a dot below the line. The 6-inch characters were seriffed in gold, shaded in black.

In March 1911 a drawing was prepared showing a new simplified style. The same two main colours were retained, but the elaborate lining was replaced by a single yellow line, applied 3 inches from the edges of all green panels, except splashers and tops of cabsides where the distance was 2 inches. Boiler bands were green edged in yellow. Main frames above the footplate were now black. Below the footplate the colours remained as before, but without any lining whatsoever. Domes, safety valve casings, and all other brass and copper items were painted over. This simplified scheme was applied to all engines as they came through shops.

In 1913 Mr Wainwright retired due to ill-health, and Mr R.E.L. Maunsell was appointed. Due to the dual needs of wartime economy and a new train reporting system, a new livery was introduced in August 1915. Engines were now painted an unvarnished olive or 'sage' green with large yellow numerals on tanks and tenders. The earlier examples of this scheme incorporated the company initials with the numbers, but this was confusing for signalmen, and so a small cast plate was adopted. This was rectangular, carrying "SE&CR" and "ASHFORD WORKS" in very small letters below on home-built engines.

Unfortunately, the olive green did not weather well, and in March 1916 a dark grey enamel was adopted, with large 18-inch white numerals. Smokeboxes were still black, but the only colour on engines was the vermilion of bufferbeams. The dark grey weathered almost to black. This remained the standard until 1923.

South Eastern & Chatham Railway

Carriage livery was described by Mr Wainwright as a 'rich purple lake', and obviously had a great deal in common with the former SER dark claret. Sides and ends were painted 'purple lake', while droplights were varnished wood. Underframes were black and roofs were white. Mansell wheels were varnished wood with white tyres.

Lining was applied to the edges of the beading and apparently followed the practice of gold on Firsts and Composites, but yellow on Thirds and Brakes. All ventilator bonnets were lined to represent louvres, despite being flat metal. Non-passenger carriage stock followed the standard painting, but without lining.

In common with the locomotives, there was a policy of simplification and economy from about 1911. Carriage stock began to be finished in a colour described as 'red-brown' or 'light lake', as opposed to the earlier dark lake [3]. What may have happened is that some of the top coats of crimson lake were omitted from the painting process, leaving the 'purple brown' undercoat more visible.

Purple brown can usually be taken to be the colour derived from mixing Indian red with a little black.

Lettering was sans-serif in gold, blocked in red, pink and white and shadowed in black. The 3-inch company letters "SE&CR" were placed centrally on the waist, with two 2½-inch numbers arranged symmetrically at each side. Doors to luggage areas carried "LUGGAGE COMPT" or "GUARD'S COMPT" in 2½-inch letters with 3-inch initials. Full Brakes carried their company initials and numbers halfway up the top panels, rather than at the waist. Class was shown by 11-inch numerals applied to the lower door panels.

Finally, from July 1916 all carriage stock was painted umber brown, almost indistinguishable from the LB&SC carriage colour, and hence probably raw umber [4]. Lettering on the umber livery was seriffed, and class numerals were reduced to about 9 inches in height.

397
South Eastern & Chatham Railway

1 'Brunswick Green'
Carter 11
Pantone 2411C
BS 381C
'Cypress Green'

2 'Vermilion'
Carter 36
Pantone 485C
BS 4800 04 E 53
'Poppy Red'

3 'Carriage Dark Lake'
Carter 43
Pantone 490
BS 381C 452
'Dark Crimson'

4 'Raw Umber'
Carter 44
Pantone 175C
BS 4800 06 C 40

South Eastern & Chatham Railway

Wagons were 'lead colour', known to be dark grey. Roofs were white, and ironwork below the solebar was black. Lettering and numbering was in 7-inch white sans-serif characters, "SE&CR" being on the bottom left plank, and the number opposite. The load to be carried was painted on the left of the solebar, and tare was painted on the right. Latterly, some open wagons carried the load painted in 6½-inch characters on the top plank, and all wagons had the number painted in 5¼-inch numerals on the bottom plank of each end.

During the Maunsell period, the dark grey was perpetuated, but was apparently applied to the whole wagon, wheels included. Lettering increased in size to 12 inches in the form "SECR". The number was in 6-inch numerals to lower left and load to lower right, but the end numbers were omitted.

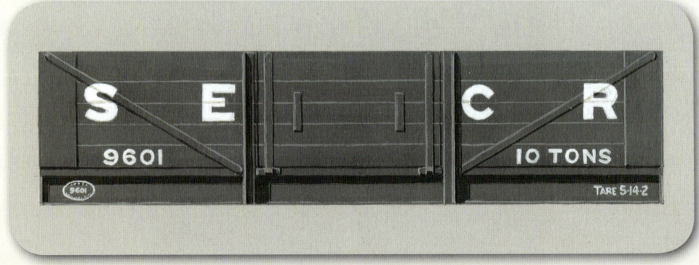

Later wagon lettering.

South Eastern Railway

The South Eastern Railway obtained its Act as 'The South Eastern & Dover Railway' in 1836 to connect the ports of Kent with London via Redhill, Tonbridge and Ashford, reaching Folkestone in 1843 and Dover in 1844. The railway purchased Folkestone Harbour and built a branch down to it.

The SER was authorised to use the London Bridge terminus of the London & Greenwich Railway and to share the route into London with the London & Brighton and the London & Croydon railways. South of London, the arrangement was that the L&BR would build the line between Croydon and Redhill, and the SER would use it free of tolls, with the option to refund half of the construction costs to claim half of the line. In 1844 the SER did just that, paying the L&BR £340,000 and claiming ownership of the line from Coulsdon to Redhill.

To avoid the London & Greenwich Railway, the SER opened its own terminus at Bricklayer's Arms in 1844. This was only open for passengers until 1852, but remained thereafter as the SER's major London goods station. In the event, the SER was able to lease the L&GR from January 1845, removing any objection to using London Bridge.

The companies worked so closely together that for a short period they pooled their locomotives and rolling stock in a Joint Committee. However, the Joint Committee was wound up on 31st January 1846, and the L&BR and L&CR amalgamated to form the London Brighton & South Coast Railway in July of that year.

The SER continued to expand in Kent and south-east London, reaching Canterbury (where it absorbed the 1830 Canterbury & Whitstable Railway) and Margate in 1846. A new line to Gravesend and Strood was opened in 1849. A branch to Reading, penetrating into Great Western Railway territory, was opened in 1849, and in 1852 a line to Hastings was opened, creating a shorter route than that of the LB&SCR.

Years of monopoly induced complacency, which allowed the East Kent Railway to establish itself in 1853, renamed the London Chatham & Dover Railway in 1859. The LC&DR opened an alternative route to Dover in 1861. This direct competition prompted the SER to extend from London Bridge to new termini at Charing Cross (1864) and Cannon Street (1866), and to construct a shorter main line to Tonbridge via Sevenoaks (1868).

The commercial rivalry between the two railways was exacerbated by the personal enmity between the two Chairmen; Edward Watkin of the SER and James Staats Forbes of the LC&DR. The rivalry only ended when Watkin resigned in 1894 after a damning report on the state of the railway in *The Investor's Review*. His successors,

2-2-2 No. 72. Author's collection

400
South Eastern Railway

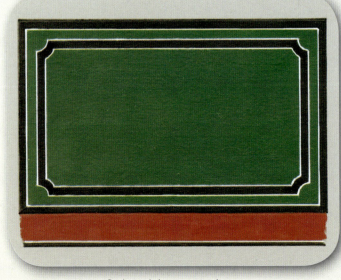

Cudworth locomotive livery.

most notably Mr Henry Cosmo Orme Bonser, improved relations so significantly that from 1st January 1899 the South Eastern and Chatham Railways Joint Managing Committee was formed, known operationally as the South Eastern & Chatham Railway.

The SER established its own engineering works at Ashford in Kent. The first Locomotive Superintendent was James I'Anson Cudworth (1845-76), followed by James Stirling (1878-98). In between were two temporary appointments: A.M. Watkin (1876-77) and Richard Mansell (1877-78).

On 31st December 1898 the SER owned a mileage of 382 miles, with a further 28 miles of leased and worked lines, and 15½ miles of joint lines. Although jointly managed as the SE&CR, the SER retained its legal identity and became a constituent of the Southern Railway in 1923, passing into the Southern Region of British Railways in 1948.

South Eastern Railway

Under Mr Cudworth, passenger engines were a medium-dark chrome green [1]. Boiler bands were black, and body panels were edged in black, both fine-lined in white. On the cab side panels (or 'fenders') and the bunkers of the well-tank engines were panels of black lining with incurved corners, fine-lined on each side with white. Tenders were divided into three or four panels by black edging following the lines of rivets, within which were more bands of lining with incurved corners. Driving wheel splashers were usually open to show the spokes, and were edged with one or sometimes two wide brass beadings.

Below the platform (footplate) the outside frames of the engine and tender were red-brown [2], described as Indian red or 'dull red'. The frames were edged in black and fine-lined in white. Wheels were green with black tyres, fine-lined on the inner edge with white. Some axle box fronts were polished brass, but others were red-brown edged in black and white. Bufferbeams were vermilion [3], edged with black and fine-lined in white. Buffer casings were vermilion, lined around the outer lip.

Outside cranks and coupling rods were polished steel, and there was a great deal of polished metal around the whole engine. Domes and safety valve covers were polished brass, as were the fillets between the boiler, smokebox and firebox. Until 1865, Cudworth engines were built with tall chimneys having a flared polished copper cap. After that time, a simple, tall stovepipe was provided.

Engines carried a modestly-sized elliptical brass numberplate with raised borders and a central number. Above the number was "SOUTH EASTERN RAILWAY" and below was the builder's name, for example "ASHFORD WORKS". Some outside builders put their works number between the name and the engine number. The plate background on the green engines was apparently black.

The position was usually on the cab fender or the bunker of the well-tanks, and it was outlined by black and white.

Goods engines, which by the end of the Cudworth period consisted mainly of his own design of 0-6-0, were a dark olive green, called at various times 'sea green', or 'a bilious green', with red-brown frames. Lining consisted of plain black banding, with incurved corners as usual. Some very old engines nearing withdrawal were painted unlined black and were known as 'coal engines'.

In 1876 Mr Cudworth could not agree the future needs of motive power with the operating department under Alfred Mellor Watkin, the Chairman's son. Edward Watkin, displaying his usual autocratic lack of tact, went to John Ramsbottom of the London & North Western Railway for advice, without Cudworth's knowledge. Mr Ramsbottom recommended that twenty of his 2-4-0 type of engine should be ordered. Mr Cudworth naturally tendered his resignation. He had the last laugh, as the 'Ironclads', as they were nick-named, were poor engines and soon relegated to secondary duties.

Alfred Watkin was appointed Locomotive Superintendent. Unfortunately, at the time he was campaigning to become Liberal MP for Great Grimsby in contravention of his terms of employment, so he was forced to resign in September 1877. Richard C. Mansell (the Carriage and Wagon Superintendent) had to step in pro tem, until James Stirling was appointed in March 1878.

Four new classes of engine appeared in this period: the 'Ironclads' mentioned above, the 'Folkestone' Class 0-6-0Ts, already designed by Mr Cudworth, the Mansell 0-4-4Ts, christened 'Gunboats', and a Mansell 0-6-0 goods engine. The tank engines displayed the usual SER livery habits, even to dividing the tankside of the 'Folkestone' tanks into three panels of lining, with incurved corners, the numberplate being central. The 'Gunboats' had tanks divided into two panels of lining, the inner verticals skirting around the perimeter of the numberplate. The domes were polished brass.

Mr Stirling ushered in a new era, introducing modern locomotives to the SER, with inside frames and proper cabs. At first he maintained the Cudworth green livery, seen on his Class 'O' 0-6-0s of 1878, Class 'A' 4-4-0s of 1879 and Class 'Q' 0-4-4Ts of 1881, but gone were the fussy multiple panels of lining. Tanks and bunkers were now lined in one large panel of black fine-lined in white, although still with incurved corners, and tenders were lined with two panels.

It was not until December 1883 and the introduction of his Class 'F' 4-4-0s that Mr Stirling made a change to the livery of new engines. The first Class 'F' (No. 205) ran on trials painted in workshop grey, but on 18th December emerged from the paint shop in a brand new livery of black. The rest of the class, and all subsequent Stirling classes, were black.

The Ashford painting records indicate that after all the usual surface preparation, filling and rubbing down to a smooth finish, four coats of dark lead colour were applied. Two coats of black followed, then lining, and finally two coats of hard-drying body varnish.

The black was originally lined out in vermilion only, involving a line edging each panel and boiler band, and then a pair of lines forming bands on tanksides and tenders, with incurved corners. Wheel tyres and centres were fine-lined with vermilion. The brass numberplates on black engines now had a vermilion background, and there were also plates on the rear of tenders. From about 1889, and certainly by 1891, the lining was supplemented by a thin yellow line applied just inside the bands formed by the pair of red lines. This became normal practice on most black engines.

The 'F' Class 4-4-0s were the first engines to feature the armorial device, placed upon their driving wheel splashers. The SER device featured a shield carrying the white horse of Kent, above which was the half-lion half-ship of the Cinque Ports. The crest was a representation of Dover Castle. The garter, carrying the name of the company in gold characters, was blue on coaches but buff on locomotives. The motto below the shield read "ONWARD".

Meanwhile, the remaining engines of Mr Stirling's predecessors (about a third of the stock by 1895) retained their former green and red-brown livery even after rebuilding, although tenders were now lined out in two panels only, and tanks in one.

One engine, 'F' Class 4-4-0 No. 240 built in February 1889, was specially prepared for the International Exhibition of that year, held in Paris from May to October. It was painted a dark brown, referred to as 'umber'. On the driving wheel splasher, the armorial device was replaced by the name "*ONWARD*" in gold lettering, curved in an arc. On returning to Kent in January 1890, the engine was repainted in black without the name, although it ever afterwards carried the gold medal that it had won.

In 1896, there seems to have been a change of heart at Ashford. Green made a reappearance on the Class 'F' engines built in that year, and on the older Class 'A' 4-4-0s receiving attention at Ashford. This was faithfully recorded in *Moore's Monthly Magazine* of June 1896. The green was described as 'medium', and it is clear that the new green was not quite the dark green of previous years. The 'B' Class 4-4-0s appeared in July 1898 painted this medium green, and by then many other engines had received the new livery, including tank engines and goods engines. The *Locomotive Magazine* by now called it 'the standard green'.

The new green livery was applied to all the engine above the platform. The smokebox, chimney, cab roof, splasher tops, platform and main inside frames were black. The valance and outside frames of tenders were red-brown, described as 'dark red'.

The beading that edged the splashers and the top and bottom of the tender flare were painted black. The cab sheets, driving wheel splashers, coupling rod splashers and tender sides were edged in more black, fine-lined in vermilion. On each panel, about half an inch inside this vermilion line was a yellow one. The tender flare seems to have been lined in yellow only. Wheels were green with black tyres, black edging to the wheel centres and black axle ends. This was all fine-lined with yellow.

Boiler bands were black, fine-lined with vermilion, with a fine yellow line on the boiler clothing about half an inch on each side. The device was applied to the driving wheel splasher, and in the case of the Class 'B' 4-4-0s also centrally on the side of the tender. The Stirling safety valve seating was now polished brass.

In addition, tenders and tanks were given a wide band of black lining fine-lined on each side with vermilion, with the traditional SER incurved corners. Tanks had one panel, but tenders were divided into two panels by this lining, the inner verticals on the tenders of the Class 'B' 4-4-0s skirting around the perimeter of their central device. Finally, about half an inch within each panel was another fine line of yellow.

The brass numberplate was still fixed to the centre of tanks, on the lower cab side sheets, or on the rear splashers. The background to the raised brass lettering had now apparently become crimson.

South Eastern Railway

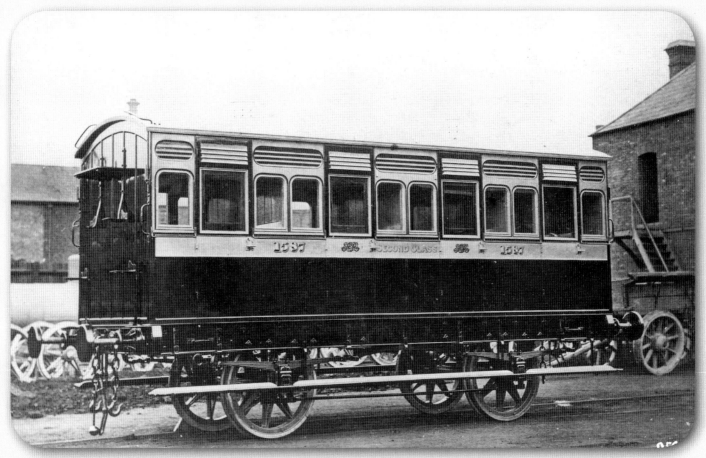

Four-wheeled Second class carriage No. 1587 in two-colour livery. *Author's collection*

Bufferbeams were vermilion edged with black, but the fine-lining was now yellow.

The green itself is a matter of conjecture. It has been said that an experimental 'Prussian green' was used, a blue-green which allegedly faded badly. Sources conflict on how this Prussian green was made. It seems likely to have been 'Alizarin' green, a green lake which was misnamed and not actually alizarin at all. What is clear is that the cleaners did not like it as it showed up every oil splash.

The first Carriage & Wagon Superintendent at Ashford was Mr Richard C. Mansell, well-known for inventing the wood-centred Mansell wheel, but he seemed unable to provide a reasonable degree of comfort for the more humble passenger, or to standardise his rolling stock.

Carriages were painted in a two-colour livery. Prior to 1874, the bottom quarter panels, carriage ends and solebars were painted a rich brown known as 'Wellington' brown. Waist panels (if present), the upright panels and the upper fascias were painted a light colour, described as 'flesh tint' or 'light salmon', in other words a buff colour. From 1874, the brown was superseded by 'dark lake' [4], the dark crimson that became the standard SER and SE&CR colour. Brake vehicles did not have side duckets, but roof 'observatories', a feature that survived on the railway until the Grouping. Brake ends were painted vermilion.

The late 1870s brought a sudden improvement in carriage design, prompted by the appearance of the SER's first bogie carriages in 1878. These carriages had a new panelling style which owed much to the contemporary carriages on the L&NWR, in that there were no waist or eaves panels as such, except on the doors. At this stage, carriages had arc roofs, but much higher and more curved than formerly. The 6-wheeled vehicles produced from 1880 onwards followed the same pattern.

In April 1882, Mr Mansell's successor William Wainwright was appointed. He changed the specification so that from 1883 carriages were painted dark lake all over. He also took the new Ashford design and developed it with a semi-elliptical roof, standard on all construction from 1888. Oil lighting also gave way to gas lighting.

The specification for the 'dark lake' was one coat lead colour, two coats purple brown, one coat rose pink and two coats best crimson lake. Carriage ends and droplights were also painted dark lake. After writing and lining carriages were given three coats of varnish.

Lining was a gold band around the fascia with a thin vermilion line edging the gold on the outside. The ventilator bonnets were no longer louvred but plain, but they were always painted dark lake and lined with gold lines as if they were louvred. The old square-framed Luggage Brake vans were lined with vermilion only.

Lettering in the Wainwright period was generally in sans-serif 2½-inch characters in gold, blocked in red, pink and white, shaded in black. Class marking was in words "FIRST", "SECOND" and "THIRD" in the waist panels of the doors. Other lettering was placed at the bottom of the upright panels, in line with the class

404
South Eastern Railway

marking. A symmetrical arrangement of two numbers spaced equally from the centre point of the carriage was preferred. On Firsts, Seconds and Composites the armorial device was applied halfway up the upright panels, usually centrally on each vehicle, or if this was not possible, two were positioned between the outermost compartments at each end. A central position was preferred for the initials "S E R", but if that was not possible the initials appeared twice, again symmetrically.

Solebars for 4- and 6-wheeled carriages would almost certainly have been dark lake originally. They were lined with a yellow line in a panel, following the perimeter of the solebar but about 1 inch in from the edge. By the 1890s, with the use of steel solebars and flitchplates, solebars were eventually painted black. An unusual feature was the notification of lubrication type above each axlebox, almost invariably being "OIL" in about 1½-inch white letters.

Even though the lot of the ordinary SER passenger had improved immeasurably, the company were still very conscious of their First class passengers. In 1891 they imported from the Gilbert Car Co., USA, several First class Drawing Room cars for the Hastings service, and in 1897 ordered from the Metropolitan Carriage & Wagon Co. a complete train of vestibuled cars for the 'Folkestone Vestibule Limited'. All these cars were typically American in outline, with clerestory roofs dressed off at each end, and end doors. The bodies were painted the standard dark lake but were elaborately decorated with gold lines and filigree work. Along the top of the body above the windows in bold seriffed gold characters was "SOUTH EASTERN

405
South Eastern Railway

RAILWAY". The type of car was painted in the bottom panels, centrally for the Gilbert cars, but at each end of the Folkestone cars. All lettering was shaded in red.

William Wainwright died in 1895, and his son Mr Harry S. Wainwright, already Works Manager, succeeded him as Carriage & Wagon Superintendent.

The ordinary London commuter was not forgotten in this period, and many sets of close-coupled suburban carriages were built between 1894 and 1899. They were all 4-wheeled to permit them to run on the City Widened Lines, and they were comfortable and well-liked. Most were electrically lit. They were painted standard dark lake, with vermilion brake ends and white roofs. The numbers, two to each carriage, and the initials were all to the standard size.

The four-compartment Firsts and First/Second Composites had a central "S E R" spaced out on adjoining panels, but the five-compartment Thirds had two closely-spaced "SER" on each side of the central door. Class marking was in large 12-inch numbers applied to the bottom door panels.

The wagons of the SER were rather archaic, and bore a close resemblance to those of its neighbours the LC&DR and the LB&SCR. Particularly noticeable were the high rounded ends of many of the open wagons, the vertical outside framing of vans, and the enclosed goods brake vans. A universal feature on SER goods stock was the use of Mansell wheels.

By 1878, and very probably from the earliest times, SER wagons were painted 'light red', the lightest pigment in the iron oxide series.

406
South Eastern Railway

Above: Brake Third No. 347.   Author's collection

Left: Position of device on carriages.

It was manufactured from calcined yellow ochre. Body ironwork, buffer casings and brake levers were black, as was all below the solebar. Brake vans were a darker red brown (Indian red or possibly brown oxide) with vermilion ends, including headstocks and buffer guides. Roofs were apparently light grey.

Lettering was white, using seriffed characters, with "SER" to the lower left of vans and open wagons, and the number to lower right, all about 7 inches high. The number was painted again in 3-inch block numerals on each end just above the drawhook. Load and tare were painted in 3-inch block characters on the solebar. Brake vans had white lettering "S.E.R GOODS BREAK" and the number below, all shaded in black.

Wagon sheets were very distinctive. They were marked with red stripes in a cross from corner to corner and from end to end along the middle. Initials and the number were on each side in about 12-inch seriffed characters, repeated in smaller (about 6-inch) plain characters at each corner. The number occurred again near the centre of the sheet.

407
South Eastern Railway

1 'Cudworth Green' Carter 16 Pantone 3537C BS 381C 226 'Mid Brunswick Green'	**2** 'Indian Red' Carter 29 Pantone 483C BS 381C 448 'Deep Indian Red'
3 'Vermilion' Carter 36 Pantone 485C BS 4800 04 E 53 'Poppy Red'	**4** 'Carriage Dark Lake' Carter 43 Pantone 490C BS 381C 452 'Dark Crimson'

Acknowledgments

Barry Railway	Cliff Harris	Rhondda & Swansea Bay Railway	Robin Simmonds
Cambrian Railways	Tony 'Dusty' Miller	Rhymney Railway	Jonathan David
	The late Mike Morton-Lloyd	Taff Vale Railway	Tony Miller
Mersey Railway	Ian Walker	Wirral Railway	Ian Walker
Midland & South Western Junction	Mike Barnsley	WM&CQR	Mark Hambly

Bibliography

British Railway Postcards of Yesteryear (Ian Allan, 1991)

North Eastern Record (3 vols) (HMRS, 1995-2000)

Railway Mechanical Engineering (2 vols) (Gresham Publishing, 1923)

Barnsley, M., *Midland & South Western Junction Railway* (2 vols) (Wild Swan, 1991)

Barrie, D.S.M., *The Barry Railway*, (Oakwood Press, 1962)

Barrie, D.S.M., *The Brecon & Merthyr Railway* (Oakwood Press, 1991)

Bolger, P., *An Illustrated History of the Cheshire Lines Committee* (Heyday Publishing, 1984)

Carter, E.F., *Britain's Railway Liveries, 1825-1948* (Starke, 1952)

Casserley, H.C., *Britain's Joint Lines* (Ian Allan, 1968)

Casserley, H.C., *British Steam Locomotives* (Warne, 1980)

Casserley, H.C. & S.W. Johnston, *Locomotives at the Grouping* (4 vols) (Ian Allan, 1966)

Chadwick, G.F., *North Staffordshire Wagons* (Wild Swan, 1993)

Coates, N., *Lancashire & Yorkshire Railway Wagon Diagrams* (L&YRS, 2000)

Comfort, N.A., *The Mid-Suffolk Railway* (Oakwood Press, 1986)

Connor, P., *The London Underground Electric Train* (Crowood Press, 2015)

Conolly, W.P., *Pre-Grouping Atlas and Gazetteer* (Ian Allan, 1958)

Crawley, J., *Great Northern Railway in Focus* (Wharton, 2001)

Dow, G. & R.E. Lacy, *Midland Style* (HMRS, 1975)

Essery, R.J., *Midland Railway Wagons, an Illustrated History* (2 vols) (OPC, 1980)

Essery, R.J. & D. Jenkinson, *Midland Railway Locomotives, an Illustrated Review* (Wild Swan, 1988)

Essery, R.J., D.P. Rowland & W.O. Steel, *British Goods Wagons: From 1887 to the Present Day* (David & Charles, 1970)

Fenwick, K., *Great North of Scotland Railway Carriages* (Lightmoor Press, 2009)

Geddes, H. & E. Bellas, *Highland Railway Liveries* (Pendragon, 1995)

Gordon, W.J., *Our Home Railways* (Warne & Co., 1910)

Gould, D., *Carriage Stock of the SE&CR* (Oakwood Press, 1976)

Hamilton Ellis, C., *The Trains We Loved* (Allen & Unwin, 1947)

Hamilton Ellis, C., *The Midland Railway* (Ian Allan, 1953)

Harvey, J., *Southern Style, Vol. 1: London & South Western Railway* (HMRS, 2014)

Hopkins, K., *North Staffordshire Locomotives* (Trent Valley, 1986)

Jenkinson, D., *The Big Four in Colour, 1935-50* (Pendragon, 1994)

Jennings, A.S., *The Modern Painter and Decorator* (3 vols) (Caxton Press, 1921)

Jeuda, B., *The Knotty* (Lightmoor, 1996)

Kidner, R.W., *The Cambrian Railways* (Oakwood, Press 1992)

Kitchenside, G.M., *Railway Carriage Album* (Ian Allan, 1966)

Lacy, R.E. & G. Dow, *Midland Railway Carriages* (2 vols) (Wild Swan, 1984-86)

MacIntosh, J., *Caledonian Railway Livery* (Lightmoor, 2008)

Maseklyne, J.N., *Locomotives I Have Known* (MAP, 1980)

Mountford, E.R., *The Barry Railway: Locomotives, Carriages and Wagons* (Oakwood Press, 1987)

Nock, O.S., *The South Eastern & Chatham Railway* (Ian Allan, 1961)

Prattley, R., *Locomotives of the Hull & Barnsley Railway* (HMRS, 1997)

Quick, J., *Robinson's Locomotive Liveries on the Great Central Railway* (Lightmoor Press, 2013)

Rush, R.W., *North Staffordshire Railway Locomotives and Rolling Stock* (Oakwood Press, 1981)

Rush, R.W., *Furness Railway, Locomotives & Rolling Stock* (Oakwood Press, 1987)

Rush, R.W., *Locomotives and Rolling Stock of the London Tilbury & Southend Railway* (Oakwood Press, 1994)

Simmons, J., *Maryport & Carlisle Railway* (Oakwood Press, 1947)

Slinn, J.N., *HMRS Livery Register No. 2: GWR* (HMRS, 1967)

Slinn, J.N., *Great Western Way* (HMRS, 1978)

Snowden, J.R., *Metropolitan Railway Rolling Stock* (Wild Swan, 2001)

Talbot, E., G. Dow, P. Millard & P. Davis, *LNWR Liveries*, (HMRS, 1985)

Tavender, L., *HMRS Livery Register No. 3: L&SWR and SR* (HMRS, 1970)

Taylor, B., *The Stratford upon Avon & Midland Junction Railway* (2 vols) (Lightmoor, 2017-18)

Weddell, G.R., *LSWR Carriages* (Kestrel, 2005)

Whitehead, R.A. & F.D, Simpson, *The Colne Valley & Halstead Railway* (Oakwood Press, 1988)

Williams, G., *The Elegance of Edwardian Railways* (OPC, 1994)

Williams, M., *Caledonian Railway Carriages* (Lightmoor, 2015)

Wisdom, P.J., *Southern Style, Vol. 2: London, Brighton and South Coast Railway* (HMRS, 2016)